Politics and the Art of Commemoration

Memorials are proliferating throughout the globe. States recognize the political value of memorials: memorials can convey national unity, a sense of overcoming violent legacies, a commitment to political stability, or the strengthening of democracy. Memorials represent fitful negotiations between states and societies symbolically to right wrongs, to recognize loss, to assert distinct historical narratives that are not dominant.

This book explores relationships among art, representation, and politics through memorials to violent pasts in Spain and Latin America. Drawing from curators, art historians, psychologists, political theorists, holocaust studies scholars, as well as the voices of artists, activists, and families of murdered and disappeared loved ones; *Politics and the Art of Commemoration* uses memorials as conceptual lenses into deep politics of conflict and as suggestive arenas for imagining democratic praxis.

Tracing deep histories of political struggle and suggesting that today's commemorative practices are innovating powerful forms of collective political action, this work will be of great interest to students and scholars of international relations, Latin American studies, and memory studies.

Katherine Hite is the Frederick Ferris Thompson Professor of Political Science and Director of the Latin American and Latino/a Studies Program at Vassar College in Poughkeepsie, New York. She is the author of *When the Romance Ended: Leaders of the Chilean Left, 1968–1998*, as well as several works on the politics of memory.

Interventions

Edited by Jenny Edkins, Aberystwyth University and Nick Vaughan-Williams, University of Warwick

As Michel Foucault has famously stated, "knowledge is not made for understanding; it is made for cutting." In this spirit The Edkins–Vaughan-Williams Interventions series solicits cutting edge, critical works that challenge mainstream understandings in international relations. It is the best place to contribute post disciplinary works that think rather than merely recognize and affirm the world recycled in IR's traditional geopolitical imaginary.

Michael J. Shapiro, University of Hawai'i at Mãnoa, USA

The series aims to advance understanding of the key areas in which scholars working within broad critical post-structural and postcolonial traditions have chosen to make their interventions, and to present innovative analyses of important topics.

Titles in the series engage with critical thinkers in philosophy, sociology, politics and other disciplines and provide situated historical, empirical and textual studies in international politics.

Politics and the Art of Commemoration

Memorials to struggle in Latin America and Spain

Katherine Hite

Routledge
Taylor & Francis Group

LONDON AND NEW YORK

First published 2012
by Routledge
2 Park Square, Milton Park, Abingdon, Oxon OX14 4RN

Simultaneously published in the USA and Canada by Routledge
711 Third Avenue, New York, NY 10017

Routledge is an imprint of the Taylor & Francis Group, an informa business

First issued in paperback 2013

British Library Cataloguing in Publication Data
A catalogue record for this book is available from the British Library

Library of Congress Cataloging in Publication Data
Hite, Katherine.
  Politics and the art of commemoration: memorials to struggle in
  Latin America and Spain/Katherine Hite.
  p.cm.—(Interventions)
  Includes bibliographical references and index.
  1. Memorials – Political aspects – Latin America. 2. Memorials –
  Political aspects – Spain. 3. Political violence – Latin America –
  History – 20th century. 4. Spain – History – Civil War, 1936–1939
  – Monuments. 5. Collective memory – Political aspects – Latin
  America. 6. Collective memory – Political aspects – Spain.
  7. Politics in art.
  I. Title.
  F1408.5.H47 2011
  980.03–dc23   2011021098

ISBN: 978–0–415–78071–1 (hbk)
ISBN: 978–0–203–15684–1 (ebk)
ISBN: 978-0-415-84354-6 (pbk)

Typeset in Times New Roman by
Florence Production Ltd, Stoodleigh, Devon

Contents

Figures

Acknowledgments

This book grows from deep love and respect for the many families of political militants who lost their lives in struggle. From my first trip to Chile as an undergraduate student almost thirty years ago, where I listened to the women of the *Agrupación de Familiares de los Detenidos–Desparecidos*, through subsequent years of testimonies, marches, organizing, solidarity, colleagueship, and friendship in several countries of Latin America and Spain, I have been profoundly educated and moved by family members.

Politics and the Art of Commemoration is also crafted very much with my undergraduate students in mind, as I am counting on them. I particularly thank current and former student research assistants Dorien Ediger-Seto, Guillermo Farias, Luis Hoyos, Carlos Leos, Kathleen Marroquín, José Medina, Ryan Meltzer, Lissette Olivares, Adriana Pericchi, and Ricardo Sánchez. Adriana was crucial to the last stretch. I also thank my Vassar senior seminar of the fall of 2009 and a follow-up independent study with Katie Aspell, Dorien, Ivana Milij-Stralj, Daniel Ming, Sarah Potts, and Austin Saddlemire, as well as Katie Jensen, Albert Mulli, Emily Thompson, and Tulio Zille. And I thank my "first students" Jan Bindas-Tenney, Adrina Garibian, Eliza Hardy, and Sarah Shanley Hope, who continue to be such important presences in my life.

For financial support for the research trips to Latin America and Spain, I thank the Elinor Nims Brink Fund, the Suzanne Schrier Heimerdinger Fund, and the Vassar Research Committee of Vassar College. The ladies of CRSR Designs in uptown Kingston, New York provided a quiet space for me to finish the writing. I also thank Routledge Intervention series editors Jenny Edkins and Nicholas Vaughan-Williams, as well as Nicola Parkin, Charlotte Hiorns, and Jane Fieldsend, for their support of this book. Beyond her role as my editor, Jenny's work on memory has very much influenced my own thinking.

I am grateful to memory muses Elizabeth Jelin, Isabel Letelier, Elizabeth Lira, and Marita Sturken. For the chapter on the *Valley of the Fallen* of Spain, I especially thank Paloma Aguilar, Margaret Crahan, Jesús Cuéllar, Guillermo Fesser, Javier Fesser, Katie Halper, Eric Hershberg, Jan Müller, and Judy Rein. Regarding my work on Peru's *The Eye that Cries*, I am indebted to Renzo

Aroni Sulca, Jo-Marie Burt, the late Carlos Iván Degregori, Gam Klutier, Cynthia Milton, Lika Mutal, Rosa Narváez, Aldo Panfichi, and Kimberly Theidon. For the chapter on the *Paine Memorial* of Chile, I so appreciate Felipe Agüero, Carolina Aguilera, Manuela Badilla, Josefina Bilbao, Cath Collins, María del Carmen Feijo, Josefina Guzmán, Alfredo Joignant, Peter Kornbluh, Juan Pablo Letelier, Juan René Maureira, Jorge Saavedra, Gabriela Ortiz, Martín Rodriguez, and Alexander Wilde. And for the chapter on the *bicis* of Argentina, I particularly thank Marcelo Brodsky, Rubén Chababo, Gonzalo Conte, Fernando Traverso, Patricia Valdez, Carlos Vilas, Mónica Vitola, and Mariana Zinni.

I thank Vassar colleagues and close friends who have commented on and supported crucial dimensions of my work: Michael Aronna, Light Carruyo, Lisa Collins, Andy Davison, Bill Hoynes, Carol Jarvis, Tim Koechlin, Beth McCormick, Himadeep Muppidi, Lisa Paravisini, Molly Shanley, Patricia Turner, Nicolás Vivalda, and Eva Woods. Throughout my memorial explorations (and well before), Jeanette Quinn Honigsbaum, Nancy Kricorian, Eliana Loveluck, Cynthia Sanborn, and Monique Segarra have accompanied me, literally and figuratively, over many, many years. Nicole Andrews, Bryant Andrews, Evry Mann, and my CCE family have helped to keep me happy and straight about what's important in life.

It is clear that the companionship of my artist in residence Robert Hite had a deep influence on my turning to the aesthetics as well as the politics of memorials. And our children Aidan and Adeline know more about memorials than most young people probably should. Fortunately, all three also have a very good sense of humor.

Finally, I thank my father, Dick Roberts, who read every sentence of the manuscript. While he could be a tough editor, and at times we agreed to disagree, he was unbelievably supportive, enthusiastic, and loving. I dedicate this book to him and to the grassroots memorial makers.

An earlier version of Chapter 2 appeared as "*Valley of the Fallen*: Tales from the Crypt," *Forum for Modern Language Studies Special Issue on European Monuments* 43 (2), 2008, 110–127.

An earlier version of Chapter 3 appeared as "*The Eye that Cries*: The Politics of Representing Victims in Contemporary Peru," *A Contra Corriente* 5 (1), Fall 2007, 108–134.

1   Memorials to struggle

My sympathies lie deeply with the former Chilean president Michelle Bachelet (2006–10). Perhaps it is because she is a woman and she introduced gender parity to the cabinet. I am moved by her identity as a socialist who lost cherished loved ones, murdered by the Chilean dictatorship (1973–90). The reaction to Chile's democratically elected president Salvador Allende's socialist experiment (1970–73) was violent and intense, unleashed through the mid-1970s and into the 1980s against leaders and militants of the left with whom Bachelet was aligned and, in some cases, intimate. Early in her presidency, Bachelet championed an agenda in consonance with the principles of those she lost, those who she remembers. In her final months in office and as a legacy of her presidency, Bachelet inaugurated a national museum of memory. She attempted to embrace a belief that families, lovers, and comrades did not die in vain.

Why has the question of memory, and in particular memories of struggle, war, conflict, and violence, exploded with such force today? It is certainly in part because memory is constitutive of who we are and how we interpret the here and now, and for many, many people, the here and now is deplorable. As a US Latin Americanist, I am mortified by the United States' continued imperialist interventions, which are all too familiar as echoes of US actions in Latin America over the past century-and-a-half or more.[1] As the daughter of US socialist parents and grandparents, I represent the most recent of at least three generations of struggle and dissent, the memories of which inform my analysis and action as well as my anger and despair.

We rely on memories to orient our understandings of the present. Collective memories, or social memories, are connective tissues.[2] US academics trace contemporary paramilitary cultures, such as the extreme rightist Minutemen, or abortion clinic bombers, to Vietnam veteran militarism and alienation.[3] We ask if Iraq or Afghanistan is another Vietnam in part because we experience the razing of homes and the killings of Iraqi men, women, and children, the incursions into Afghani villages, the unmanned missiles into Pakistan, as we might remember the carpet bombings, devastation, and killings of more than a million Vietnamese. Returning US veterans of Iraq and Afghanistan, physically and psychologically maimed from their actions, recall the continued national failure to care properly for returning GIs.[4] Eight more Iraqis killed, another US missile explodes in a Pakistani village. We are incessantly reminded of utterly senseless violence and loss both present and past. In our search for explanations of what, exactly, went wrong, and how we became so unmoored, so powerless, we become melancholic, nostalgic, and reflective.[5] We ask where meaning lies in the current wreckage, as well as what our children will face as we continue to dig a deeper morass.

In this book, I explore the politics of commemoration as a lens into the ways people attempt to make meaning of violent political memories, particularly the loss of loved ones in political struggle. Traditionally states have attempted to commemorate the past while projecting unity, peace, and purpose, often in the aftermath of atrocious violence in which states are deeply implicated. Official commemorations often take the form of monuments, which, as distinct from memorials, emphasize a victorious past over mournful, contemplative loss or sacrifice. But increasingly today we are also witnessing all kinds of society-driven efforts, in creative tension and negotiation with the state, to establish memorials, and to memorialize that which both challenges state violence and insists on alternative global imaginaries. Further, in a global context in which technologies of representation and communication are rapidly evolving, collectivities are innovating memorial making. In addition, "counter-memorial" movements have also sprung up internationally, both to mourn the dead and to spur political mobilization. These multiple efforts raise questions crucial to debates on the politics of memory regarding grief, empathy, and collective action that are now in constant flux.

Historians constantly debate the degree to which the present impinges on interpretations of history.[6] Yet there is no doubt that memory profoundly informs how we understand the current juncture, and that our memories are a moving target in relation to an ever-changing present. There is a powerful dynamic between our memories and our identities. Traumatic memories deeply mark individuals and collectivities; traumatic events resonate well into the future.

The difficulties of integrating traumatic losses are hindered by political contexts that attempt to dehumanize violence and by some cultural contexts in which grief is seen as a private matter, best contained, hidden. In wars, armed conflicts, and in political repression, states inflict violence in ways in which the human consequences are often made to seem somehow divorced from the damage. Those left to grieve the dead are often expected to do so in private, perhaps in an honorable military funeral service, or amidst a fearful, even hostile political milieu that suspects their loved ones were complicit in their own demise.

In many, though by no means all, cultures, there is often a way in which grieving, particularly prolonged grief, is seen as self-pity and, therefore, as unacceptable. Joan Didion captures this sense of her society's expectation that the aggrieved should heal quickly, that after the initial shock and the funeral, those who grieve should be on the road to recovery, to meaning, again.

Instead, Didion writes that it is "the unending absence that follows, the void, the very opposite of meaning, the relentless succession of moments during which we will confront the experience of meaninglessness itself."[7]

Didion wants her readers to allow for, to begin to understand, perhaps even to empathize with what serious grief might mean for those intimately experiencing such grief. While she might say that we as the non-aggrieved must grant time and space for the fragility, the instability of the griever, she also challenges us to take a close look at how we judge the aggrieved.[8]

Our distance, numbness, or our implicit insistence that others' grief take place behind closed doors, borders uneasily on complicity, on enlarging the void rather than on imagining how we might begin to fill the void, through collective mourning. Struggles to integrate traumatic memories and events in revolutionary and affirming ways constitute essential tasks for our sense of selves and our communities, as well as for our activism toward the possible.

In Judith Butler's essay, "Violence, Mourning, and Politics," she urges us to imagine a global community built on shared mourning, on the assumption that all human life is equally precious and valued.[9] Butler poses the challenge to the US citizenry to embrace an alternative, non-violent response to the violence of September 11, 2001. She approaches the theoretical task from a deliberate acknowledgment of the enormity of US force, in its many iterations. Such force, Butler argues, includes the capacity to harm significant swathes of humanity, and, therefore, requires our acceptance of responsibility for such harm. If we respond to the loss of human lives in New York City, Washington, DC, and Pennsylvania, with deadly force abroad, Butler suggests, then we accept that lives in one part of the world are inherently less worthy of life than our own. Butler strives to have us absolutely reject some "hierarchy of grief," to empower mourning, toward a globalizing "recognition" of one another.[10]

Politics and the Art of Commemoration examines the questions of empathy, grief, and mobilizing through four sites of commemoration—the first an intensely statist project led by General Francisco Franco in the aftermath of the Spanish Civil War; the second a fitful commemorative process in Lima, Peru, that emanated from an artist's abstract sculpture to mourn violence; the third a multigenerational grassroots-initiated memorial in one community of Chile; and the fourth a stenciled image that began as a commemoration of the disappeared of Rosario, Argentina, and has since traveled the world to assume distinct memorial meanings. I suggest that memorials can be cathartic and empowering as well as conflictive, in ways that are unanticipated as well as anticipated, as catalysts for political dialogue, solidarity, and action.

I focus on four major memorial sites as portals into the complicated politics of struggle. Certainly other cases abound. Spain, Argentina, Chile, and Peru are not alone in sharing histories of intense political conflict, authoritarianism, repression, and transition from authoritarian rule. These four sites were chosen because of the distinctive and different ways they bring out the political and social subjectivities of the memorials' protagonists, commemorative representations, and conceptual concerns, which together provide tremendous insights regarding the power and promise of the politics of commemoration.

I grew up in a radical US left household, where the dynamics of both historic and contemporary international revolutionary parties and struggles were a central part of our conversation. Coming from a family whose party politics were so marginal to US power intrigued me to places in the world where the organized left was not so marginal. I became immersed in intense study, activism, and human rights work on the US and Latin America, and I grew close to and was inspired by many activists, including those who lost loved ones. In performance theorist Diana Taylor's *Disappearing Acts*, Taylor is constantly interrogating her own and others' subject positions as they represent the horrors and resonances of places other than our own, in Taylor's case, Argentina's brutality under the 1976–83 dictatorship. Taylor worries that we are voyeurs, or worse, that we are "capitalizing on the suffering endured by others—for reasons that might include the need to establish a sense of cultural superiority over the violent 'other' or for professional advancement."[11] I appreciate her concern. I understand my study of the politics of commemoration in Spain, Peru, Chile, and Argentina as intimately linked to my political biography and activism, to US imperial might and complicity in the violence, and to a commitment to grieve, honor, and respect the dead and to be attentive to the living.

Commemoration as transformative

The politics of commemoration recognizes that commemorative processes are more than symbolic exercises to acknowledge the past. Memorialization can transform the meanings of the past and mobilize the present. States are born of violence and produce and reproduce violent, major trauma. There is, therefore, a state logic, often aided by a loyal citizenry, to doing the re-memory work of structuring a nation, of shoring up nationalism or patriotism in order to build state stability and represent the state in a non-violent, even glorious way.[12] Rather than remembering the violence of war for what it was, conquering and claiming territory, killing and maiming, building armies and state coffers that are war "chests," states use language and representations to reframe the violence as something other than violence.[13] States adopt a language, a historical memory narrative that says we *bought* the island of Manhattan from the Indians, that we *purchased* Louisiana, that we *settled* the western frontier, and so forth.

Clearly, much official memorial work is essentially representing an image of a unified, strong state, particularly in the aftermath of major violence, such as war, where the state conscripts young men and women into the army to fight, to die, to be wounded, to sacrifice, for some purpose of state, and often with at least the initial consent of its citizens, who only have some of the story, or who have been lied to about the extent of the threat, or who really believe war can achieve security and victory. So it is all the more important in the aftermath of war to reclaim the nation and those who have died in service to the state, to convey a message of respectful thanks that nonetheless masks, or erases, or does gross injustice to the myriad stories and lives of those lost, the questions of "for what?" or "how could it be?"[14] As the US continued its brutality and destruction in occupied Iraq, it was no surprise that the Bush administration prohibited the showing of the coffins, the dead bodies of the US soldiers being returned to their families. The prohibiting was an explicit erasure, an attempt to control or at least to limit the questions and the gravity of violent loss.

Photographs, video footage, images, and symbolic representations are potent tools of politics, even if it is difficult to gauge exactly how they come to bear on public opinion. Walter Cronkite's valiant efforts to bring Vietnam into people's living rooms played a profound role in helping to shift US society's turn against the war. Dramatic images stay with us and can be mobilizing. This was the case with Eddie Adams's Pulitzer Prize-winning 1968 photograph of General Nguyen Ngoc Loan executing a Viet Cong militant, or Sam Nzima's 1976 photo of ten-year-old Hector Pieterson being carried dead in another young man's arms during the Soweto, South Africa uprisings. At the Hector Pieterson Museum of Soweto today, curators have fashioned a powerful narrative of anti-apartheid resistance from the grassroots, launching almost entirely from that photographic image.

Throughout Latin America and elsewhere, families have used photographs of the faces of their disappeared loved ones to press politicians into action, to struggle to determine their loved ones' whereabouts, imprinted with the question/demand, *"Dónde está?"* Relatives have covered their hearts with the photographs, marched in silence, risked their own lives, chained themselves to fences, outed former torturers, and made memorials. The photographs are indexes, both markers and traces, once produced at least in part by the person who is now the object, whose image has now become a sign, a banner, an emblem, a conscience.[15] As discussed in Taylor's *Disappearing Acts*, the photographs of the *desaparecidos* evoke a lost, often youthful humanity, both haunting and at the same time accessed, claimed, and even iconicized by the viewers.[16] The young faces evoke sadness, anger, and shock as viewers contemplate their fates. The photographs are powerful tools of political mobilization.

In Susan Sontag's prescient analysis of the power of an emblematic photograph, one forever etched in our minds, Sontag captures a photograph's commemorative capacity: "Strictly speaking," Sontag writes,

> there is no such thing as collective memory—part of the same family of spurious notions as collective guilt. But there is collective instruction ... What is called collective memory is not a remembering but a stipulating: that *this* is important, and this is the story about how it happened, with the pictures that lock the story in our minds.[17]

Photographs of the missing young people of Argentina, Chile, Peru, and elsewhere, are now displayed in exhibits and museums, harnessed in official spaces of collective instruction, locking the stories in.

The power of symbolic structures, such as memorials, can be more ambiguous. Yet the demand for memorials has increased dramatically. Memory scholar Elizabeth Jelin characterized this phenomenon as a "fever for memorialization."[18] Once virtually the sole domain of states as patrimonial claimants, memorials are now championed by an enormous range of political and social groups who seek representation across a multiplicity of identities.[19] Grassroots organizations are constructing memorial exhibits to visualize their claims and demands. To mourn the havoc and loss in Iraq, for example, the Quaker-based non-governmental organization the American Friends Service Committee (AFSC) has organized memorial exhibits around the country. The AFSC's *Eyes Wide Open: The Costs of War* uses the boots and shoes of dead US soldiers and Iraqi civilians, as well as photographs from Iraq to craft the exhibit. At each exhibit site, local organizations, churches, and schools lay out the boots. *Eyes Wide Open* has traveled to forty-four states.[20] Similarly, in Santa Monica, California, each Sunday from sunrise to sunset, another NGO, Veterans for Peace, organizes a temporary memorial of coffins, crosses, and mementos from lost soldiers' family members. The memorial project is called *Arlington West*.[21] The number of coffins each Sunday is determined by the week's losses in Iraq and Afghanistan.

As part of a longstanding tradition of weaving and quilt making to represent loss and to bring women together toward a collective purpose, the anti-war women's group CodePink established the Peace Ribbon Project.[22] Like the AFSC project, the Peace Ribbon traverses communities of the US, and women gather to weave patches of quilt in memory of US soldiers and Iraqi civilians killed in Iraq. As discussed in Chapter 3 regarding a similar weaving project in Peru, the Peace Ribbon Project represents a form of empathic unsettlement; that is, an artistic representation that on its surface is beautiful, bright, and multiple and yet in its unfolding and our contemplation takes us into the horror of violence and trauma.[23]

Clearly, the increased demands for symbolic representation cannot be equated with a number of other pressing forms of redress, and memorials cannot be a substitute for social justice. Yet memorials have the power to make visible, literally, a social consciousness, to assert a message, to catalyze a necessary conversation. The *Arlington West* project specifies that education and dialogue are crucial objectives of the memorial. *Eyes Wide Open* structures in discussions as well as contemplative and deliberate silence in the Quaker tradition. Memorials can awaken, challenge, and mobilize their observers, in some instances in a dialogic relation to the memorial makers, in others through deliberative contemplation of the memorials themselves.

We know that many memorials actively engage only those who are most intensely connected to them, namely the family members and loved ones of those the memorials directly represent, as well as others on the ground who have struggled to establish them. This is not to say that memorials that are deeply meaningful to the families of those whose names are inscribed or who are in other ways directly represented are not in and of themselves quite important. As Chapter 3 analyzes, in Lima, Peru, families of the disappeared from around the country come periodically to mourn at *The Eye that Cries* sculpture. What some had initially dismissed as too abstract a representation became a cherished memorial, fiercely protected by relatives of the Peruvian dead and disappeared, so many of whom have no body to bury, no graveside to go to grieve. The sculpture acts as a meeting place, where many of the relatives recount that they feel their loved ones' presence.[24] Family members engage in what Jenny Edkins has termed an "encircling" of the trauma, that is, they use memorials to bring linear time (i.e., the fact that a loved one was disappeared in some recent past) together with trauma time (where the disappearance of their loved one is never past).[25] As described further below, *The Eye that Cries* is designed to invite such an encircling.

Like other visual objects, certain memorials attain more than symbolic representation and communication. Agents infuse memorials. Memorials can become a means of acting; they can possess transformative power.[26] If we understand that memorials are embedded in social relationships and historical–political contexts, then memorials are relational nodes presenting the past, acting and acted upon (and against) by individuals and collectivities. Memorials such as *Eyes Wide Open* and *Arlington West* do reach out to many publics to evoke what Michel Foucault has called "the solidarity of the shaken,"[27] those moved to empathy by the making visible of the many deaths.

From monuments to memorials

Monuments champion grand projects or leaders, they herald past greatness. Memorials, more broadly, commemorate the past in ways that recognize sacrifice or loss. Art critic Arthur Danto distinguishes monuments from memorials:

> We erect monuments so that we shall always remember and build memorials so that we shall never forget. Thus, we have the Washington Monument but the *Lincoln Memorial*. Monuments commemorate the memorable and embody the myths of beginnings. Memorials ritualize remembrance and mark the reality of ends.[28]

We often use the terms interchangeably, though we tend to associate monuments, at least subconsciously, with intensely masculine, erect physical structures, such as the Washington Monument, or the Voortrekker Monument to the Dutch-descended Boers of South Africa, or any number of statues of famous men, standing tall or on horseback. This is also very much the case with Spain's the *Valley of the Fallen*, discussed below. Not surprisingly, and though I cannot claim to command hard data on this, there seems to be less monumentalizing and much more memorializing going on these days.

In the US, the break with monumentalizing, including its masculinist dimensions, and the resurgence of academic as well as public interest in memorials are widely attributed to Maya Lin's 1982 Vietnam Veteran's Memorial.[29] Her design and the memorial's execution defied convention, as a horizontal, minimalist structure. The V-shape of the memorial wall cut into the ground's natural surface. When Lin's design was chosen, detractors loudly denounced the selection as a disservice to the veterans. They claimed the memorial represented a scar or a wound, that its V-shape emasculated the soldiers.[30] Critics demanded and secured a second, representational memorial sculpture next to the wall. Yet no one anticipated the deeply moving engagement that the *Vietnam Veterans Memorial* would evoke. Veterans and families who lost their loved ones pour out their grief, trace their loved ones' names, and place letters, flowers, and mementos.[31] Visitors not directly connected to the veterans find themselves profoundly touched by the memorial.

Inherent in the power of the *Vietnam Veterans Memorial* is its invitation to sorrowful reflection. As we follow the wall, we travel inward, below the ground, becoming enveloped in an overwhelming sense of sadness as we face the sheer numbers of names and study the mementos placed along the wall's floor. As we read the names we also see ourselves projecting from the polished granite, eliciting greater inward reflection.

Lin's design, her deliberate reach for visitors' inward searching, has become deeply influential. The 1995 *Korean War Veterans Memorial* to the one-and-a-half million US soldiers who fought, 54,000 of whom died, draws quite consciously from Lin's conception of the wall. It is located at one point of a triangle with the *Lincoln Memorial* and the *Vietnam Veterans Memorial*. Cooper-Lecky architects created a granite photomural that similarly achieves its visitors' reflections, here in relation to digitally reproduced images from Korean War archives rather than dead soldiers' names. The wall's photographs convey faces of men and women who appear uncertain, apprehensive. The wall also reflects back to the viewer the nineteen larger-than-life, gray stainless steel representational sculptures of soldiers who are positioned opposite the wall. The soldiers are meant to be climbing a hill, their faces tense, watchful, even fearful. There is a reflecting pool at one end of the wall that triangularizes the wall and the sculptures. Like the *Vietnam Veterans Memorial*, the *Korean War Veterans Memorial* emphasizes somber contemplation over celebration.

Lin's influence is also quite clear in the design and construction of the recently inaugurated memorial wall, the *Monument to the Victims of State Terrorism* in the Memory Park of Buenos Aires, Argentina.[32] The wall commemorates and names approximately 9,000 Argentines who "disappeared" and were murdered by the brutal dictatorship from 1976–83. The Memory Park and Monument ties the great River Plate, the estuary dividing Argentina from

Figure 1.1 Detail of *Monument to the Victims of State Terrorism*, Memory Park, Buenos Aires, Argentina (photo by Katherine Jensen).

Uruguay, to the city, and the city to a national trauma of the repression and the killings, as well as to the global context.[33] To give a sense of the Monument's scope and texture, as well as its parallels with the *Vietnam Veterans Memorial*, I cite Holocaust and memory studies scholar Andreas Huyssen's description of the Argentine memory wall design at length:

> the monument cuts deep into the elevated grassy surface of the park that faces the river in the half round. It is like a wound or a scar that runs the full diameter of the half circle in zigzag formation from the straight line of one walkway toward another paved path that frames the whole length of the park at the shore . . . The open view toward the river is a key element in the design, which is classically modernist in its geometric configuration and felicitously minimalist in its lack of ornamentation and monumental ambition. It is thoroughly imbued with an aesthetic sensibility but never approaches the risk of aestheticizing traumatic memory. In its stylized simplicity of design it offers a place of reflection to its visitors.[34]

Like the *Vietnam Veterans Memorial*, the process of constructing the Argentine memorial wall was similarly fraught. There was a great deal of debate concerning what the inscription on the main rock at the entrance to the monument should read—the debate focused on what the victims had struggled for and toward what ends their fates. In the end, the sentence reads: "This Monument is established in homage to the victims of state terrorism and to the ideals of freedom, solidarity, and justice for those who lived and struggled." There were also debates about how to ensure that the order in which the names are recorded on the stones privileges forced disappearances as the dominant repressive methodology.

Although ten leading Argentine human rights groups participated in the process of elaborating the entire project, not all human rights groups supported the Memory Park and Monument initiative. Particular groups protested at the inauguration of the first rock, including one prominent faction of the Madres de Plaza de Mayo, some members of the Association of Ex-Detained Disappeared, and HIJOS (a group of children of the disappeared). They accused the legislators and political party members of belonging to the same political forces that had voted in favor of legislation that had given impunity to crimes of the dictatorship. Hebe Bonafini, leader of one prominent faction of the Madres, resisted the "individualization" of the 30,000 victims that placing names would symbolize, that this would offend "our revolutionary loved ones." She threatened to attempt to erase physically the names on the stones.

The inauguration of Argentina's Wall of Memory took place in November 2007. Hundreds gathered and both President Nestor Kirchner and his wife, then future president Cristina Fernández, presided over the inaugural ceremony. According to colleagues and two of my students who attended the inauguration, the divisions among the human rights organizations over the design and scope of the park and the memory wall were not visible, and the ceremony was quite moving.[35] Unlike the Vietnam memorial wall, however, the Monument to the Victims in Buenos Aires is hardly visited or even widely known to Argentines.

Memorials' reach, their potential to make broad publics aware of their existence and meaning, depends on locations that are easily accessible and on the agents who engage them. In April 2007, I visited *Women in Memory*, a memorial in the center of Santiago, Chile. Before my visit, I read through the transcript of the inauguration of the memorial, which took place on the evening of December 12, 2006, the day former Chilean dictator Augusto Pinochet was cremated. The ceremony was reported to have been beautiful and extremely moving, and the images of the memorial on my laptop screen were luminous, taken at night, displaying the memorial wall of granite and crystal, wonderfully lit, with fresh-cut roses at the foot.

Women in Memory was the initiative of twelve women, including former political prisoners, exiles, and relatives of the murdered women. It took four years and the contributions of dozens of grassroots organizations and individuals in Chile and abroad. Many gathered for the inauguration; the youth orchestra of Paine, Chile, composed of grandchildren, nephews, and nieces of the detained—disappeared, performed a moving piece, women sang, and feminist intellectual and activist Sandra Palestro gave a powerful speech.

Figure 1.2 Monument to the Victims of State Terrorism, receding to the River Plate (photo by Katherine Jensen).

Palestro described the ways women raised support for the project, and she thanked women in government, women from community-based organizations, women well known and not so well known. Palestro emphasized that while the memorial commemorated the 118 Chilean women killed by the junta, seventy-two of whom remain disappeared, it was also a memorial to women killed throughout Latin America, from Ciudad Juárez, Mexico, to Guatemala, El Salvador, and Argentina. *Women in Memory* is proclaimed as the first memorial of its kind.

When I arrived in Chile four months after the inauguration, I began asking friends where the *Women in Memory Memorial* stood, exactly. Most had no idea. One got on his cell phone to consult a friend "who should know." No luck. My close Chilean friends are left-of-center, politically astute, and involved. Yet they were unaware that such a memorial existed. I called a former political prisoner. He somewhat embarrassedly confessed that he had been out of the country for the inauguration and had not visited the memorial and could not be completely confident regarding the memorial's exact location.

Back in my hotel room I searched the memorial's location online. It stands at the crossroads of the Pan American Highway and the Alameda Bernardo O'Higgins, the busiest street of Santiago. The memorial is above Los Héroes metro station, one of the most traveled convergence points of the Santiago subway system. I set out on the Transantiago metro, deciding to disembark one stop before Los Héroes in order to visit the presidential palace and the Salvador Allende monument. I then walked the eight or so blocks down the Alameda. I kept looking to my left, to the center of the thoroughfare, to catch my first glimpse of *Women in Memory*. Unwittingly, I passed it. I turned my head back and realized my mistake.[36]

With the assistance of some construction workers' instructions, I managed to make my way to the thoroughfare, edging along the narrow walkway bordering the site. I found the steps up to the memorial, over an entrance to the subway station. And there it was. At the top of the steps, there is a small plaque imprinted with the title and the three governmental and non-governmental sponsors. As I began to walk toward the memorial itself, I stopped short, startled. Seated against the memorial, with all his possessions by his side, was a homeless man. It was a hot afternoon, and he was shirtless, occasionally pouring a bottle of water over the top half of his body to cool himself down. I maintained some distance, as it was clear we were both uncomfortable with my presence. I smiled and said hello but received no reply. I snapped some pictures, from further away than I had wished. Here was a memorial to women, including Chilean revolutionary women murdered in the 1970s by the dictatorship, women fighting for a world free from inequality and injustice. More than thirty years later, here is this man. The utter, painful irony was inescapable.

Figure 1.3 Women in Memory Memorial, accompanied by a homeless man,
Santiago, Chile (photo by Katherine Hite).

A few days after my encounter with the memorial, I left Santiago in the wee hours of the morning, when all was still dark. My taxi driver took me down the Alameda to the airport. As we drove by Los Héroes, I glanced back, and the memorial was lit up, and it was absolutely beautiful. The idea that this memorial was a failure now seemed too absolutist, too dismissive. By day I had questioned the eerie parallel between the revolutionary women's agendas and the memorial itself as failed projects. The homeless man seemed to drive home the structural violences of contemporary Chilean inequality, far more disparate today than over thirty years ago. I was shaken that day by the imagery that flashed through my mind of the ways Chilean female political prisoners were tortured, brutalized, turned into horrendous shadows of their former selves, murdered, disappeared. And I could not help but stare at the memorial, scratched with some graffiti, surrounded by litter, and inhabited by a homeless man, and wonder, had the women died in vain? Is this how we honor them? Yet with darkness as her backdrop, *Women in Memory* achieved a luminescent, haunting effect, accomplishing her intent. The memorial was clearly retrievable.

The Maya Lin-influenced memorial walls have shaken up conventional funerary memorial designs that list names and dates in a kind of generic recording of soldiers' deaths.[37] These many years after its 1982 inauguration, the *Vietnam Veterans Memorial* continues to evoke a profound response from her visitors. Yet it is also clear that the *Vietnam Veterans Memorial* is exceptional. Many, many memorials have been forgotten. In the past, certainly, the process of securing a major memorial was always conflictive, contested, but once the memorial went up, there seemed to be a way in which the marking accomplished its task, and the memorial became just another stone on the road to somewhere else. Pierre Nora argued that states erected monuments precisely in order to forget, to claim a mission accomplished.[38] Today, however, the politicization of both monuments and memorials on a world scale is detectable, and Nora's general claim does not hold.

Counter-monuments/Counter-memorials

With innovations in the ways atrocities are represented, linking powerful representations to genocidal political issues, the *Vietnam Veterans Memorial* captured in the public imagination the conflicts and loss Vietnam represented. In the context of the immense makeover of nations and cultures that globalization has effected and its politicization of memorials, it is not surprising that a counter-memorial movement has also arisen to shake up conventional commemorative rites and representations.

In a recent Vassar College class seminar on coming to terms with mass violence and atrocity, we discussed the *Vietnam Veterans Memorial*, including how profoundly the memorial touches those who visit. Several students expressed similar sentiments of being moved as they recalled their visits to the memorial with family or as part of a middle school or high school field trip. Yet one student said she remembered "not really getting what the big deal was," that she honestly "couldn't relate" to the memorial, and other students in the class were relieved that someone braved this comment, for they had felt the same way. The most striking contribution of the discussion, however, came from two students who said they had been talking about the assigned memorial reading the night before, and what they wanted to know was, "Where are the Vietnamese in this memorial?"

The class discussion drove home the challenges of creating a meaningful memorial for a range of publics, as well as the elusiveness of a memorial's staying power over generations and distinct historical–political junctures. On the one hand, my students reflect a generation whose exposure to visual imagery, often to many images at once, as both analysts and consumers, has made them discerning and often quite sophisticated critics. Accessing emotion or feeling through a dark, staid memorial of polished granite proved difficult, even alienating. For them, a certain numbness, or cynicism feels almost structured into a funerary design.

In addition, students in my class have been exposed to postcolonial debates. They have learned to look for the power dynamics that shape what account of history is emphasized or told, and they are attentive to the silences and erasures that empire invariably entails, even in the context of mourning human loss, human tragedy.

This frustration with the ways memorials often have little meaning, or somehow let states and societies off the hook for egregious violence, is central to the motivations behind what Holocaust memorial scholar James Young has termed a "counter-monument" movement. The movement evolved during roughly the same period as Maya Lin's emergence and work, and movements have proliferated throughout the world. Young attributes the roots of the counter-monument shift to German artist Jochen Gerz, who began showing, or sometimes performing, distinct counter-monuments in the 1970s.[39] Gerz's intent has been to expose into full public view the tendency of Germans to "exercise a sort of sublime repression of the past." Gerz seeks "to turn this relation to the past into a public event."[40]

Not allowing society to forget is central to the concept of counter-monument makers. On March 24, 2000, the twenty-fourth anniversary of the Argentine coup, the Rosario, Argentina, artist collective En Trámite launched its first major public art installation, *Descongesta*. As Figure 1.4 illustrates, the piece was composed of old pairs of shoes embedded in forty blocks of ice. The artists placed the piece on a corner in front of a former center for clandestine detention and torture that was converted into a fancy bar. As the ice blocks melted in the hot sun, the ice formed pools of water on the sidewalk and then evaporated altogether, leaving the shoes sprawled along the pavement. "Nothing more inoffensive than a puddle on the sidewalk," the artists claimed. "A flash of memory to anesthetize the coldness of forgetting, to chill the pain."

After close study and consistent participation in the traditional com-memoration of September 11, 1973, the day of Chile's brutal military *coup*

Figure 1.4 Descongesta, melting blocks of ice, Rosario, Argentina (photo by
    Fernando Traverso).

d'état, a group of university students organized "MarchaRearme," a march to
"re-arm" or re-signify the ritual. The social psychology students perceived that
the September 11 march from the presidential palace to the memorial wall of
the detained–disappeared and politically executed in Santiago's General
Cemetery had become stagnant, defeatist, emphasizing the death and
victimization of members of the Chilean left, rather than the protagonism of
those who died while struggling to construct a new society.[41] To counter the
"walk of defeat," students began their march from the General Cemetery and
carried reproductions of the names inscribed on the memorial wall to the
presidential palace. MarchaRearme inverted the traditional march, bringing
out those in the cemetery. The counter-commemoration also sought to open
the ritual to broader sectors of Chilean society, as well as to other
interpretations of the past.[42]

   In Peru, the Peruvian Forensic Anthropology Team (EPAF), which over
the past several years has been exhuming mass graves of those killed
during the 1980–2000 internal armed conflict, announced an "Open Up Your
Umbrellas!" campaign. EPAF and other Peruvian human rights organizations
sought "to sensitize the citizenry regarding the humanitarian demands of
more than fifteen thousand families of disappeared persons during the conflict.
Such demands focus on the necessity of being able to find their loved ones
and bury them with dignity."[43] The campaign drew from the images of families
of the disappeared in the Andean highlands, standing in the rain under their

Figure 1.5 At the start of the counter-commemorative march, "MarchaRearme,"
        Santiago General Cemetery, Santiago, Chile (photo by Evelyn Hevia).

umbrellas, observing the work of the forensic team. People gathered together
in a plaza and performed what the EPAF bulletin termed a "flash mob," a
somewhat ironic twist on a popular marketing strategy. EPAF translates "flash
mob" as a "simultaneous multitude," "an organized action in which a large
group of people gathers freely and all-of-a-sudden, in a public place to do
something unusual and then rapidly disperse." This group opened their
umbrellas.

   Coordinated chiefly through the internet, including social media, and word
of mouth, this lightning-like action entreated observers—either passers-by or
those who caught an image in the press—to be surprised, to wonder, and to
want to know more. A friend who lives in Lima and who received an email
about the pending flash mob said to me that she thought the choice of umbrellas
was odd, given it never rains in Lima and many people don't own umbrellas.
She had trouble imagining how this could be effective. Yet the organizers were
media-savvy, the imagery appeared in newspapers and on television, and clearly
enough participants came armed with umbrellas in order to achieve an eye-
catching moment of brightness.

   In the context of the elusiveness, the uncertainty of the staying power of
some of the most evocative memorials, counter-monument movements, and
commemorations such as these are intriguing. They remind us there is no
such thing as permanence in time or space, and perhaps more importantly,

no such thing as closure on traumatic memories. The Argentine block of ice, the Chilean MarchaRearme, and the Peruvian flash mob involved small collectivities of cultural workers, activists mobilizing counter-memorials that capture imaginations, that (re)awaken a public conscience, if only for a moment.

Counter-commemorations also prove unsettling, exemplified by an awkward exchange I had with a student during the fall of 2008. The student was recounting her summer working for a US Democratic congresswoman and her dismay when a group of women anti-war activists staged a several-day-long, counter-commemorative "die-in" on the floor of her boss's office. The student felt that the die-in targeted the wrong representative given her boss's progressive politics, and that it was largely characterized as a group of crazy women who interfered with the important business at hand. I countered that there was another famous group of women who had similarly been termed, "*las locas*," the crazy women of Argentina—the Mothers of the Plaza de Mayo—who bravely confronted the military dictatorship to demand to know the whereabouts of their loved ones. I said that the CodePink women staged the die-in because they deeply believe one more death from US war or occupation is unacceptable.

It was clear that the student did not find my explanation convincing. It did, however, open up a conversation about the culture of detachment, insulation, even cynicism that enmeshes congressional office staffers, who become embroiled in defending particular pieces of legislation and denouncing other pieces, who answer phone calls and letters from constituents they never meet, and who find that even a Girl Scout visit can be an annoying distraction from the rhetoric-crafting, paperwork, and conversations that are the "more important" work of the US congressional representative staff. The student did admit that the memories of the counter-commemorative die-in will continue to bother, and perhaps haunt her, for some time to come.

In one of the most extreme cases of designing a distinct kind of counter-monument given what we know about both the circularity and impermanence of meanings over time and space, a US government-commissioned group was assigned the task of designing a warning marker for a major nuclear waste dump in New Mexico. As art historian Julia Bryan-Wilson recounts, a group of "anthropologists, linguists, archaeologists, and engineers" is attempting to develop a "marker to survive the next ten millennia while continually broadcasting its message of danger with no slippage or decay or meaning."[44] It is both a fascinating and an eerie endeavor.

The deep politics of memorials

Even the most imposing, enormous state monuments face the inevitability that time is destructive to intention around memory of painful pasts. The Spanish dictatorship of Francisco Franco (1939–75) carried the state erasure of massive violence through symbolic representation to new heights. The *Valley of the*

Fallen is Spain's largest public monument, located roughly thirty miles from Madrid. It is solitary and fortress-like. The main feature is a cross towering over a crypt, consecrated in 1960 by the Pope as a Basilica. The crypt burrows directly into rock as an unshakeable, eternal edifice that is both lodged into and elevated above the earth.

The monument harnesses centuries of political, religious, cultural, regional, imperial conflict into a dramatic statement on the victory, asserting that western Christianity will triumph over all. It is a physically formidable, even massive memorial, a symbolic effort to control and to retrieve time. And yet, despite the tremendous resources deployed to erect and maintain the monument, to lodge a particular rendition of history forever into the landscape of Spain, the *Valley of the Fallen* has come under scrutiny as a one-sided interpretation of the past, at best, and a gross injustice, at worst.

In an important contribution to postcolonial politics of memory debates, Michael Rothberg argues that we must pay a great deal more attention to what he terms the "multidirectionality" of memory, that is, the connections across time and place among mass atrocities.[45] Using the Holocaust as his anchor, Rothberg traces the particularity of the Holocaust while establishing the links of the Holocaust to racist, imperialist state aggression by the French state against Algerians.

After many, many years of official Spanish silence regarding the *Valley of the Fallen*, the monument has erupted into an important point of political debate. In 2007, the Spanish parliament passed a historical memory law that demands, in part, that the *Valley of the Fallen* represent "both sides" of the civil war. Families, including grandchildren of those who fought on the side of the Republic and are buried in the crypt, are now demanding their grandparents be exhumed and reburied in sites that honor their memories. The *Valley of the Fallen* as a monument, as a site of memory, has become a point of departure for current debates in Spain about the past and how the past should be remembered or suppressed, but also, in more hidden, fraught ways, how the past can be understood in relation to current debates and tensions surrounding the questions of empire, colonialism, and immigration.

The quest for empathy constitutes a central preoccupation surrounding controversy on the Peruvian memorial, *The Eye that Cries*. In dramatic contrast to the *Valley of the Fallen* as a grand state project, artist Lika Mutal's sculpture mourns centuries of colonialist violence. The *Valley of the Fallen* and *The Eye that Cries* speak both to historic imperial aggression and violence as well as to twentieth-century ideological conflict. One is an extreme, championing enunciation of victory, vanquisher, and patriarchy, another a representation of mourning, loss, and maternal wisdom.

To center the memorial, Mutal sculpted a representation of the indigenous ancestral goddess Pachamama, Mother Earth. Mutal shaped Pachamama from an ancient, pre-Inca stone she had found on a trek in northern Peru years before, and in the stone she affixed another rock as an eye. A trickle of water runs continually from the rock, as an eye that cries, that mourns the violence.

The stone of Pachamama conveys a maternal quality of the familiarity and ongoing duress of suffering, implicitly against a notion of a masculine inflicting of violence. The representation also projects an eternal sense of victimization, neither periodizing nor romanticizing a "pre-violence" or "pre-conflict" historical moment. Mutal represents the genealogy of the victims as long and deep.

The Eye that Cries penetrates a fraught, uneasy politics in Peru regarding the reaches and limits of understanding the trauma of "the other." The vast majority of those who lived in terror and with terror were indigenous peasants of the Peruvian highlands, physically and socially quite distanced from the dominant Peruvian metropolis of Lima. In many cases, violence emanating from both the military and *Sendero* destroyed collective organization, tore families apart, and left communities of widows and orphans. When individuals and families displaced by the violence in the Andes descended to Lima, they were often viewed with suspicion and fear. Drawing from both eastern and western philosophy and spirituality, *The Eye that Cries* seeks compassion for the descendants of those who are foundational to Peruvian identity yet who are structurally marginalized from power.

Maternal loss, represented in such an abstract way by Mutal's stone of Pachamama, figures emblematically in trauma representations, in art, photography, and literature, and has become an important issue in memorialization debates. Writing about representations of the Holocaust, feminist scholars Claire Kahane and Marianne Hirsch caution us to be circumspect about the reaches and limits of the figure of maternal loss.[46] Hirsch is particularly concerned with what she has termed the "generation of postmemory," the children born to Holocaust survivors, children who did not themselves live through the Holocaust but for whom the traumatic memories are deeply formative. Postmemorial generations, Hirsch suggests, require new forms of representation. Regarding the question of memories as mobilizing, Hirsch also asks, "Can the memory of genocide be transformed into action and resistance?"[47]

The *Memorial of Paine*, Chile, brings to the fore the concerns of intergenerational transmission and mobilization of traumatic memories. Three generations of families have come together to create a unique memorial in Paine, a once rural area that is now more of a bedroom community twenty miles from Santiago. Paine was the site of intense brutality in the immediate aftermath of the 1973 coup. Until the mid-twentieth century, Paine was comprised of large haciendas and a local aristocracy. From the mid-1960s to 1973, Paine became the site of major agrarian reform. The military coup meant swift, concerted, and deadly retaliation against Paine's peasant organizers and their supporters. According to the 1991 report of the official Chilean Truth and Reconciliation Commission, more citizens per capita died and disappeared in Paine than in any other site in the country.

Visitors to the *Paine Memorial* first see a conceptual forest of timber, cut to different lengths to recall an Andean horizon. The forest is composed of one thousand individual logs, minus seventy. The missing seventy are those who disappeared or were executed from Paine. The thousand logs represent all the surviving family members. Replacing each missing pine is a family-designed mosaic to remember an individual murdered loved one. The mosaics are colorful and are filled with different imagery—tractors, watermelons, guitars, and soccer balls. Some are more abstract, with tears, or drops of blood. Some are explicitly political, with political party flags, colors, and famous party militants.

The *Memorial of Paine* has involved a volatile, and ultimately successful collaboration between the government and families of the victims to create a beautiful and inviting series of remembrances. Still a work in progress, the *Paine Memorial* contemplates space for events and regular meetings, and fully three generations of Paine citizens actively participate in the site. The grandchildren of Paine's disappeared and executed formed an activist group, "The Third Generation." The group insisted the *Paine Memorial* deliberately emphasizes life, "*una memoria viva*," living memory. Through the *Paine Memorial*, we can read both the pain of what took place and the possibility of cross-class and cross-cultural solidarity. In the long aftermath of dictatorship and suffering, we can examine the struggles and the negotiations between the grassroots and the state. The memorial uniquely expresses an imagined future as well as a somewhat idyllic past. It also represents a persistent set of demands for justice, passed through several generations.

Memorials can be mobilizing frames, mourning the dead but denying that it was all for naught. Bicycles are stenciled all over the Argentine city of Rosario. At first glance they appear real, as if they were leaning up against the side of a building or a house. The *bicis* (bikes) mark particular sites—a school, a residence, a post office, a former detention and torture center. The *bicis* are black silhouettes, literally traces, or markers, of absence. Rosario artist Fernando Traverso uses the *bicis* to symbolize the 350 or more citizens of Rosario who disappeared during the 1976–83 dictatorship, including several of his former comrades.

Citizens of Rosario know the *bicis*, yet interestingly, most have come to associate Traverso's stencil not with the *desaparecidos* of the dictatorship, but rather with the far more recent brutal killing of Pocho Leprati, a Rosarino grassroots activist known for his Christ-like physical appearance and his bicycle. Police forces killed Leprati during a major 2001 mobilization to protest the capitalist economic crisis. Leprati's memory is now enjoined with the memories of those who resisted capitalism and state brutality a generation before.

Conceived at the community and national levels, memorial making such as Traverso's has increasingly become an important component of ongoing democratization work. Continuing a rich tradition of art in the street, artists and artist collectives have used a range of urban landscapes to communicate messages of political urgency, to provoke ongoing reaction and contemplation. Together with collectivities around the world, Traverso has democratized, pluralized the reach and meanings of his *bicis*. To recognize the shared fates

Figure 1.6 Bici, door of Londres 38, former clandestine detention center, Santiago, Chile (photo by Katherine Hite).

and struggles with citizens across the Andes, a Traverso *bici* now appears on the door of a former clandestine detention and torture center in Santiago, Chile. University students in Juárez, Mexico, and El Paso, Texas, joined forces and invited Traverso to stencil *bicis* on both sides of the border, to represent movement, migration, loss, and resistance. The *bici* has appeared in many parts of Europe and Latin America as a symbol of sustainable environmental movements.

Lika Mutal's *The Eye that Cries* in Peru is an abstract sculpture inspired by her Buddhist beliefs, feminist sensibilities, and her sensitivities to relationships between ancient indigenous cultures and nature. The *Paine Memorial* of Chile is a series of mosaics and wood that depicts imagery and color of life and death, lived memory. Fernando Traverso's *bicis* are stencils of bicycles that signify movement as well as loss, that travel across the world to join global representations of struggle.

The fundamental challenge is to channel memory toward a global imaginary that eschews violence and builds solidarity and community. This is not to commodify memory, nor to relegate memory to some past condition, for memories are lived, ongoing social practices, ever in motion. This book seeks to begin to explore representations of memory as lenses into the deep politics of struggle and conflict and as suggestive arenas for imagining democratic praxis.

2   Memorializing Spain's narrative of empire

"I think we should consider blowing it up," said Basque parliamentarian Iñaki Anasagasti, in one intense Spanish legislative debate in September 2010 over what to do with the Holy Cross of the *Valley of the Fallen*—Spanish dictator Francisco Franco's enormous tomb and physical legacy, the largest monument in Spain. "Leave it to a Basque to suggest this!" stated another member of the legislature, alluding to the ETA, the Basque terrorist organization born during Franco's long reign (1939–75) as a counterinsurgency group.

There is no love lost between the Basques and Franco, who among other repressive measures suppressed the use of the Basque language, as well as the languages of Catalonia and Galicia. In 1937, in the midst of the Spanish Civil War, Nazi Germany's Condor Legion aided Franco's Nationalists in a massive aerial bombardment of the Basque town of Guernica, a devastating act memorialized by artist Pablo Picasso's masterpiece, "Guernica." The *Valley of the Fallen*, on the other hand, was Franco's attempt to memorialize a very different history.

The *Valley of the Fallen* is located roughly thirty miles from Madrid. It is solitary and fortress-like. The main feature is the crypt, consecrated in 1960 by the Pope as a Basilica. Buried in the crypt are Francisco Franco and an early Franco ally and martyr, the 1930s leader of the Spanish Falangists José Antonio Primo de Rivera, as well as approximately 33,000 citizens who fought in the Spanish Civil War (1936–39).[1] The crypt burrows directly into rock as an unshakeable, eternal edifice that is both lodged into and elevated above the earth. To reach the crypt is unmistakably like undertaking a pilgrimage along a long, lone, climbing road. Franco deliberately placed the monument in close proximity to other magisterial, imperial monuments of Spain— the Escorial, the Granja, palaces erected by past kings.

Now, thirty-five years since the death of Franco and more than half a century since the end of the Spanish Civil War, the Spanish government and society are finally confronting the atrocities of the war and the repression that followed. What had been a long, cautious transition from dictatorial rule in the wake of Franco's death in 1975 came to an end. In good part, this breaking of the silences of the past can be attributed to a thoroughly subordinated Spanish military, notable generational turnover among political elites, and a moment

Figure 2.1 Entrance to the Basilica of the *Valley of the Fallen*, Madrid, Spain
(photo by K. Rakoll).

in which prosecutors as well as activists throughout the globe are holding select
human rights violators of the past accountable.[2] Spain has joined states and
societies in Latin America and elsewhere as they face the multiply constituted
violence of the recent and not so recent past.

The legislative debate regarding the *Valley of the Fallen* represents one
in a series of fraught Spanish discussions today over the politics of commemoration. On October 31, 2007, the congress passed the Law of Historical
Memory, a comprehensive piece of legislation that includes exhuming and
reburying the remains of thousands of Republicans killed during the Spanish
Civil War; ridding the country of monuments to Franco, as well as to either
side of the civil war; compensating all validated legal claims of major human
rights abuse during the war and the dictatorship; granting citizenship to
children and grandchildren of Republican exiles; and refiguring how the
Valley of the Fallen represents the past.[3] Article 16 regarding the *Valley
of the Fallen* is vague regarding how this stipulation should be done, though
it prohibits ceremonies that "exalt" the Nationalists or the Franco regime. The
2007 law reflects the Spanish state's response to increased demands from a
growing number of civil society groups. These include descendants of those
killed defending the Spanish Republic whose family members are entombed
in the *Valley of the Fallen*'s enormous crypt.

Here I seek to explore the many meanings of the *Valley of the Fallen* as a monument, as a site of memory, as a point of departure for current debates in Spain about the past and how the past should be remembered or suppressed. I also examine how the *Valley of the Fallen*'s commemorative art—the tapestries, statues, the gigantic mosaic aligning the crypt's dome—can be understood in relation to current debates and tensions surrounding the questions of empire, colonialism, and immigration.

The *Valley of the Fallen*'s uncomfortable fit

"It's a curious place," a Spanish friend and well-known filmmaker, Javier Fesser, remarked, in a rather non-committal way, when I told him that I had begun an exploration of the *Valley of the Fallen*. "How do you think about the place?" I asked. "Frankly," Javier replied, "I hardly think about it at all." Until recently, Javier's reaction to my query was a common one in Madrid— a kind of rolling of the eyes, a sigh, a shrug of the shoulders, a seemingly detached remark about how strange and ugly the site is and how infrequently Spaniards visit there.[4]

I tried to imagine an equivalent kind of monument here in the US— something that exudes the feel of what might be the interior of an austere, threatening temple in some high forest—something that might similarly be a source of embarrassment if inquired about by a foreign visitor. I shifted my thoughts away from the actual construction of the *Valley of the Fallen* itself to imagine a more conceptual equivalent—one man's attempt to establish a monument to fellow men, God, and empire across time in a glorious, albeit violent, celebrated national past.

There are any number of monuments to US history that are both cumulative and instantiated sites of violence, sources of America's constitutive identity— civil war battlegrounds, the many plantations throughout the US south, Little Big Horn, Wounded Knee, the Alamo. Such places are not territorially bound, for, like Franco's monument, they invoke global reach and the violations of peoples within and across borders.

As Javier and I continued to talk I learned that he and his family had gone to the *Valley of the Fallen* from time to time. The monument commands a spectacular view of Madrid and includes a monastery as well as the crypt, lush grounds, and the tallest, most imposing cross in the world. For Javier, who comes from a large, Catholic family, the *Valley of the Fallen* is a tourist attraction, a place to picnic with the children. In fact, Javier attended a wedding in the crypt.

A wedding? It is a haunting space, full of bellicose sculpture and imagery, built underground, into rock, in order to inter Franco and tens of thousands of war dead, almost half of whom are anonymous.[5] What overwhelms is the austerity, darkness (a crypt, after all is said and done), and cold. The wedding Javier attended took place between a woman he worked with and a young man, also named Javier, who had been a Benedictine choirboy and had lived in the

Figure 2.2 Javier de la Fuente, former choirboy (photo by Javier Fesser).

monastery from the ages of ten to fourteen, as his father had before him. Franco had decreed that the monastery connected to the crypt would house and train at least thirty-five choirboys who would perform each day at mass, and the decree is still in effect.

In July 2005, Javier arranged for us to meet his friend Javier de la Fuente, now in his early thirties, and he took us to the monastery. It was clear that while the former choirboy and resident of the *Valley* was aware of the deep resentment harbored against the *Valley of the Fallen*, Javier de la Fuente (depicted in Figure 2.2) wished Spaniards could appreciate or at least consider the *Valley* as something other than a fascist project. "I loved my four years here," Javier said. "When our time was up, none of us wanted to leave. For me, personally, the *Valley of the Fallen* is not about fascism. It is about music."

At the monastery, Javier introduced us to the recently retired director of the choir, Father Laurentino, a Benedictine monk who together with Javier's father had been a founding choir member. Father Laurentino guided us through the cloistered monastery (including areas Javier was surprised I was permitted to enter as a woman) and the crypt. Father Laurentino had lived in the monastery of the *Valley of the Fallen* for forty-six years, having entered the seminary at the age of twelve. Unlike most of the other twenty-five monks living in the *Valley*, Father Laurentino has traveled around much of the world.

Figure 2.3 Benedictine Father Laurentino (photo by Javier Fesser).

The monk made several references to his concern regarding the "political machinations" and "lies" currently at play regarding what to do with the *Valley of the Fallen*. Laurentino said—only half in jest—that it was possible Franco was not interred in the tomb, for no one from the monastery had officially performed the custom of viewing and confirming that the body was indeed Franco's.

The exchange with Father Laurentino reflected just the beginning of the mounting tensions between the Benedictine Abbey and the Spanish state, even though until early 2010, such tensions were largely hidden from public view. In late December 2009 the government decided to shut the main entrance to the *Valley of the Fallen*, claiming that important repairs to both the structure and a statue were necessary. Religious leaders and activists affiliated with the Benedictine order cried foul, charging that the government was inventing excuses to shutter the *Valley of the Fallen*.[6] The Benedictines' eleven am mass was allowed to continue and to be attended by visitors, but those in attendance were asked to leave the basilica immediately following the service. The government faced increased questioning regarding the levels of state financial support for the *Valley of the Fallen*, as well as increased demands to alter the site's representation of the past.

In spite of expressed legislation in the Historical Memory law forbidding political demonstrations at the *Valley of the Fallen*, on November 20, 2010, the anniversary of the deaths of both Franco and José Antonio Primo de Rivera, neo-Nazis faced off at the site against members of the Association for the Recuperation of Historical Memory.[7] The latter group demanded that the cross

Figure 2.4 Father Laurentino and the author, before the Benedictine monastery (photo by Javier Fesser).

come down and that the remains of the Falangist leader and the dictator be moved to private cemeteries. The neo-Nazis ardently defended the dead leaders. On December 19, 2010, the main doors to the crypt reopened. In his announcement to the press, minister of the presidency Ramón Jáuregui admitted that while the government and the Benedictine monks had come to an agreement, "important problems" between them remained.[8]

Conceptualizing the crypt's intent

> The War of Spanish Liberation was a Crusade, as declared by Pope Pius XII. It was the representation, in the twentieth century, of the victory achieved by Don Juan de Austria in Lepanto. If the Spaniards had not stopped communism, no one today can doubt that from 1939 on the Iberian Peninsula, as a part of Europe, and possibly of America, would live as slaves of a philosophy that privileges materialism over spirituality; atheism over religion; and oppression over freedom, which in essence would mean the destruction of western civilization.
>
> ("Reasons for the Construction of the *Basilica of the Valley of the Fallen*," Francisco Franco National Foundation, 1976)

While Franco's *Valley of the Fallen* glorifies the dictator's personal legacy, the monument is also a major effort to assert a Christian–military nationalist Spain as a model to the world. The Franco dictatorship (1939–75) led Spain through gradual but nonetheless dramatic social and economic transformations. Many claim the dictatorship was a brutal, lengthy thwarting of the secular progressive, including Communist, political forces that championed the Spanish Republic (1931–39). Others see the Franco regime as central to remaking Spain into a viable, modern member of twentieth-century Europe. It seems clear that the dictatorship was both a brutal reactionary and transformative national project, enjoying the significant support of the Spanish political right, the Vatican, and the Spanish Catholic church hierarchy.

The regime also reinvigorated the Spanish military as an institution, which had fragmented and weakened in the face of significant colonial losses, namely in the Americas, but also in northern Africa. Putting the Spanish military back on the map came primarily through military officers who, like Franco, had risen through the ranks of the colonial Army of Africa based in the Spanish Protectorate of northern Morocco. In 1936, Franco's men launched the assault on the Republic from their Spanish Moroccan bases.

And finally, Franco owed his victory in large part to the support of the fascist regimes of Hitler and Mussolini, as well as to the refusal of England, France, and others, under the guise of the Non-Intervention Committee, to come to the defense of the Republic. The United States cited the 1935 Neutrality Act to justify its lack of support to the Spanish government. By all accounts, UK, French, and US non-intervention played into the hands of Franco's Nationalists and their Italian and German allies. The Soviet Union did assist the Republic, albeit weakly, as the USSR was also a party to the Non-Intervention agreement and sought to stave off its deteriorating relations with Europe. As Franco's obsessive symbolic legacy, then, the *Valley of the Fallen* represents the ultimate embodiment of the military–church–right-wing alliance, as well as the primacy of Spain as a defender of western civilization.

The Spanish Catholic church hierarchy fully supported Franco, and on April 15, 1939, two weeks after Franco's victory, Pope Pius XII congratulated Franco in a message to "heroic Spain, God's chosen nation."[9] While the previous pope, Pius XI, had been more hesitant to endorse Franco unequivocally, Pius XII saw Franco as a champion against communism.[10] Drawing from this notion of Spain as God's chosen nation, Franco imagined the *Valley of the Fallen* as memorializing the Christian struggle against the ardently anticlerical Republic, to be represented by a cathedral grander than that of Rome's St. Peter's. In fact, the original design for the crypt was larger than St. Peter's but was scaled back at the request of the Vatican. On April 7, 1960, one year after the crypt was inaugurated, Pope John XXIII formally raised the category of the crypt to that of a basilica.

The dictator further demonstrated the church–regime link by conceptualizing a role for a monastery intimately connected to the monument. Through the establishment of a Foundation of the Holy Cross of the *Valley of the Fallen* just prior to the opening of the crypt, the Spanish state forged a formal agreement with the Benedictine Abbey of Silos. The agreement entrusted the Benedictine Abbot with overseeing the crypt, ensuring daily and special

Figure 2.5 Benedictine monastery (photo by Javier Fesser).

masses, housing and educating the choirboys who would also perform at each mass, and supervising a guesthouse and a social issues-oriented library and study center.[11]

In a subsequent legal accord in which the Spanish state acknowledged it would underwrite the Benedictines, the monks agreed to hold special masses in the crypt on the days deemed holy by the regime, including: July 17, the eve of the launch of Franco's coup and "triumph of the Holy Cross"; April 1, the day of the Nationalist victory; October 1, Franco's birthday; November 20, a day to remember those who had "fallen for our Crusade," particularly José Antonio Primo de Rivera, executed by the Republicans in 1936 on this date, as well as Franco himself, whose death was declared on November 20, 1975; and the many saints days of the military.[12] Today there are twenty-six monks and forty-four choirboys who continue to carry out these dictates, and the Spanish state continues to underwrite the entire enterprise.

Franco's conception of the monument was not a simple link between church and state. The *Valley* evokes the memory of the historic Crusades. For Franco, the Crusades refer to the reign of the Spanish Hapsburg empire, to the Catholic Kings' late fifteenth-century Reconquest of Spain and defeat of an Islamic dynasty, to the expulsions and forced conversions of the Jews, and to the expansion of Spanish imperial control across the seas. As a veteran of the Spanish colonial wars against the Rifs in Morocco, which were often deemed a twentieth-century Reconquest, Franco associated his mission against the Republic as a divinely mandated ridding the nation of "foreign" elements via a twentieth-century Crusade.

Two of the men intimately involved with Franco in the crypt's conceptualization, the architect Diego Mendes and the sculptor Juan de Avalos, both claimed that they dissuaded the dictator from carrying out his vision for the crypt's walls: Franco wanted to create bas-reliefs running the length of the nave on each side of the crypt depicting the "heroes and martyrs" of the civil war as modern-day crusaders.[13] The Franco-appointed council overseeing the crypt's construction commissioned various mural-sized sketches of heroes and martyrs—heroes running one side of the nave, martyrs the other. The sketches, over 150 feet in length and done by the Bolivian artist Reque Meribia, were placed on the walls as tests. They are now housed in the General Archive at the Royal Palace in Madrid.[14]

According to the architect, Mendes understood the dictator's intent and sent for Belgian artist Guillermo Pannemaker's famous *Apocalypse Tapestries*. Commissioned by Spanish monarch Philip II in the mid-sixteenth century, the tapestries were hanging in the nearby La Granja Palace, and, incredibly, Franco had the 400-year-old tapestries carried out of the palace and into the crypt. The eight masterpieces illustrate in great detail the Apostle St. John's Book of Revelations, from the story of the Last Judgment, through the seven plagues and the destruction of man, to the armies of Christ and the triumph of Christ and the church over the devil. Mendes placed the tapestries on the walls and invited Franco and his right-hand man, Minister of Government Luis Carrero Blanco, to view them. Carrero Blanco, a foremost authority on the 1571 Battle of Lepanto and the period of Phillip II, helped to convince Franco that the tapestries better conveyed the dictator's vision of representing those who had died in Franco's grandiose conception to identify his repression with the Crusades.[15] While the architect, the sculptor, the government minister, and an archbishop apparently talked Franco out of the heroes and martyrs bas-reliefs along the nave, there is no escaping the "Crusadist" imagery from one end of the crypt to the other. Bas-reliefs of heroes and martyrs of the historic Crusades did find a place in the choir, where they are etched above the wooden pews.

The crypt's nave contains six chapels, dedicated to different representations of the Virgin symbols drawn deeply from Vatican iconography. Three of the chapels are devoted to patron saints of the military: *The Immaculate Conception*, the patron saint of the Army; *Our Lady of Mount Carmel*, patron saint of the Navy; and *Our Lady of Loreto*, patron saint of the Air Force. A fourth, *Our Lady of Mercy*, patron saint of captives, symbolizes all the prisoners whose lives were spared by the Nationalists.[16] The fifth chapel is dedicated to *Our Lady of Pilar*, patron saint of the Spanish Ebro region, site of the final, decisive battle of the war.

The binaries of good and evil, God and devil, allies and enemies, are represented throughout the monument, attempting to mask what would seem strange bedfellows crucial to Franco's victory. The meanings of the sixth chapel, *Our Lady of Africa*, merit attention in this regard. At one level, the chapel monumentalizes Franco's launching of the Nationalist struggle from the African continent. With the important assistance of German and Italian ships and planes, the Nationalists' long march essentially began from the Spanish Protectorate bases of Melilla and Ceuta, crossing the seven miles over the Straits of Gibraltar, battling through Andalusia and Extremadura to Madrid and to Republican strongholds.

Yet *Our Lady of Africa* reaches deeper, for it symbolizes a pinnacle and a turning point: In the late 1920s, after close to two decades of Spanish military defeat at the hands of Moroccans attempting to drive Spanish colonial forces from their lands, the Spanish Army of Africa had become a formidable military force. During the Spanish Civil War, Franco and his fellow Africanist officers employed a discourse that reflected experiences and lessons from the colonialist wars in Morocco, and the Nationalist military victory would not have been achieved without the Army of Africa.[17]

Following the Disaster of Anual, a crushing 1921 defeat of the Spanish army by the Moroccan Rifs, in which 8,000–12,000 Spanish soldiers lost their lives, the colonial army was rebuilt as a cohesive, conservative nationalist military.[18] By the mid-1930s, the Army of Africa had amassed a fighting force that included the Spanish foreign legion and tens of thousands of *Regulares*, or native Moroccan troops. Soldiers from the Army of Africa were deployed to suppress radical working-class revolts in Spain in 1930 and 1932. In 1933, in the historically left-wing Spanish province of Asturias, Army of Africa troops thwarted a major workers' uprising against the center-right government. This was a tactical warm-up for the Army of Africa's full-fledged deployment in the civil war.[19] Over the course of the war, an estimated 78,500 Moroccans fought on the Nationalist side. Approximately one in every eight Moroccan soldiers lost his life.[20]

Franco and his fellow leaders developed an ideological rationale—at least temporarily—in which the enemy was no longer understood as North African, but rather as the Communist infidel. Africanist officers had never exhibited religious zeal, and their colonialist stance tended to characterize Moroccans as a backward, primitive, savage race rather than as infidels. The officers exploited shared anti-Semitic bonds, calling forth an image of Jews as the instigators of the Spanish partisan left. For the Spanish nationalist veterans of the colonial wars, the new enemy would thus become the enemy within Spain, allied with the Soviet Union and Zionism.[21] In addition, the Nationalist-led Spanish foreign legion and *regulares* used particularly brutal tactics against Republican soldiers and sympathizers, including women, and such tactics traverse collective memories across generations to continue to reproduce an image of the savage Muslim Other.

At the end of the nave guarding the entrance to the transept of the crypt on each side are frightening, hooded virgins of stone representing each of the patron saints of the four military branches. On either side of the transept are the mausoleums containing the 33,000 dead. While the official guidebook states that both Nationalists and Republicans are interred at the *Valley of the Fallen*, it recognizes that the vast majority buried there are Nationalists, and that only Republicans who were proven Catholics could be interred in the crypt.

Past the hooded virgins is the gigantic dome arching over the transept. A five million-piece tiled mosaic covers the dome. The mosaic depicts the many Nationalist forces, including the Falangists, the Carlists (monarchists), and military officers, and the artist links these groups to saints, as well as Jesus

Figure 2.6 A hooded virgin inside the crypt of the *Valley of the Fallen*
(photo by K. Rakoll).

and the Virgin Mary. It may be the only cathedral mosaic in the world that features a cannon. Father Pérez de Urbel, a close adviser to the regime and author of the first edition of the official guide to the *Valley of the Fallen*, described the mosaic in grandiose terms:

> You cannot imagine a more magnificent, more profoundly expressive scene: in the center, the figure of a seated Christ surrounded by a multitude of saints sent to heaven by the churches of Spain: martyrs, virgins, doctors, kings, popes, founders, prelates and farmers.[22]

Franco and José Antonio Primo de Rivera also appear in the mosaic, though no guidebook mentions it. Rather, the official texts focus on the simple, 3,000 pound. tombstones of the two leaders, buried in the transept floor. Separating the two tombs is the altar, featuring Jesus on a cross, made from a tree trunk Franco is said to have chosen and cut down personally.

Many Francoist sympathizers denied Franco imagined himself buried in the crypt along with José Antonio Primo de Rivera and the 40,000 interred at the outset. Others, such as Diego Mendez and Father Pérez de Urbel, claim that this burial in the transept was his intention all along.[23] When Franco died, more than 35,000 ex-soldiers ascended the road to the *Valley of the Fallen* to attend the dictator's interment. The one foreign head of state in attendance was Chilean dictator General Augusto Pinochet, a Franco disciple.

Visiting the crypt

Franco envisioned the crypt would be built in a year. It would take twenty. In addition, it would take another twenty years to exhume and re-inter the remains of those now buried in the crypt.[24] The construction, exhumations, and reburials required an enormous outlay of capital and resources in a period in which they were in short supply. At the end of the war in 1939, much of the country lay devastated, and approximately 300,000 Spaniards had died violent deaths.[25] The years 1941–42 were those of the Great Famine, and severe food shortages continued through mid-decade. Agricultural production would not return to its 1930–35 levels until the late 1950s.

A reported 650,000 men and women were prisoners of the Nationalists.[26] In 1940, the year the decree for the *Valley*'s construction went into effect, approximately 234,000 men and women were being held in concentration camps.[27] Implementing a plan conceived by a Spanish priest and close Franco ally, the regime established a "doctrine of redemption": in exchange for laboring in both state and state-contracted projects, political prisoners would receive three days reduced from their sentences for each day of labor served, as well as a very small wage based on family size. Among some of the more lively debates today regarding the repression of the Franco years is the question of what constitutes "forced" labor. Throughout the 1940s and until the prison labor program formally came to a close in 1950, estimates of how many political prisoners worked on the *Valley of the Fallen* range from 14,000 to 20,000.[28] There are no reliable figures available for the many laborers who died building it. A local doctor recounted treating several fatal injuries and the prevalence of terminal lung diseases contracted in the blasting and burrowing.

The official guide to the *Valley of the Fallen* emphasizes the grandiosity, the beauty of the setting, and the remarkable feat of the architectural achievement. As of this writing, the guide and its many translations are the only written texts about the crypt available at the monument. The English translation carries one brief sentence acknowledging the fact that political prisoners built the monument. There is no such acknowledgement on the official audio listener's guide.

As of 2004, the Spanish state recorded that 407,572 visitors had passed through the crypt. The majority were foreign tourists, though there were also special groups of both Spaniards and foreigners who deeply identify with the project. In the recent past, such groups have included surviving members and descendants of the Condor Legion, the German airforce unit that in 1937 bombed Guernica. [29] Each November 20, Spanish Falangists and German and Italian fascists gather at the crypt to commemorate José Antonio Primo de Rivera (or "José Antonio" as he is known and as is recorded on his tombstone) and Franco and to denounce democracy.[30] In the face of now quite public debates about what to do with the *Valley of the Fallen*, the November 20 gatherings have attracted far larger crowds than in years past.

On the other hand, significant numbers of Spaniards have deliberately refused to visit the *Valley*. One is the well-known Spanish historian and former political prisoner/laborer in the *Valley*, Nicolás Sánchez Albornoz, who, together with his fellow university student organizer and prisoner Manuel Lezama, made a spectacular escape from the *Valley* in a car owned by Norman Mailer. Sánchez Albornoz has claimed he will not return until the monument is converted into a garage or, alternately, he has "the right to piss on Franco's grave."[31] "I would never go to the *Valley of the Fallen*," an acquaintance remarked to me. "I only say, 'Look at the big cross up there on the mountain!' when my kids and I drive past." As a devout Catholic, she is ambivalent about what to share with her children regarding the cross's context.

In addition to those who refuse to enter the crypt, there are those who have tried to blow it up, or at least a part of it. I have come across three recorded attempts, the first of which was shortly after the *Valley*'s 1960 inauguration, when a pair of French anarchists, posing as tourists, planted a bomb that they detonated four hours after they left the site. No one was injured, but the police arrested Francisco Sánchez Ruano, a young Spanish anarchist who had taken the French anarchists to the *Valley* yet had no prior knowledge of the bomb. Sánchez Ruano served eleven years in prison for a crime he did not commit.[32]

A second bombing occurred in 1999, claimed by the October 1 Revolutionary Anti-Fascist Group (GRAPO). While the bomb destroyed a confessional and several pews and left large pockmarks in the stone walls, no one was hurt. The group chose the crypt as the ultimate fascist symbol and timed the bombing to coincide with the sixtieth anniversary of the fall of the Republic.[33]

One bombing of the *Valley of the Fallen* occurred during my visit to Madrid, when *El Pais* reported that in the early morning of May 27, 2005, someone planted a "homemade bomb" under a wooden bridge in one of the *Valley*'s gardens. Officials speculated it was the work of "a person or group, but unconnected to an organized party."[34]

These bombings (and most likely others) at the *Valley* over the decades are protests against fascism and the silence surrounding the violence the monument both represents and attempts to obscure. Monuments throughout the world project and mask state violence. Citizens at the grassroots challenge the maskings.[35] As state-orchestrated monuments attempt to convey continuity, stability, and a well-ordered past to serve the present, societies periodically confront public monuments as they seek to reveal state injustices. Small but persistent groups have successfully struggled in Spain's new millennium to force the unmasking, to debate, re-think and reconfigure the *Valley of the Fallen*.

Yet monuments turn in on themselves as well. Inside Franco's crypt there are physical scars, wounds—the water from the mountains that seeps through the rock appears eerily like bloodstains, dripping through distinct areas of the crypt's walls. As Jacques Derrida expresses regarding twentieth-century struggle, loss, and a search for meaning, the ghosts of 300,000 civil war dead and 28,000 executed deny statist intent to control.[36] The dictatorship attempted to annihilate the left, the anti-clerics, the anti-monarchists—all constructed as foreigners within. Outside the crypt, silences are breaking down. Within the crypt, the ghosts are there.

Breaking the silences

On March 15, 2004, the Spanish presidential race that only days earlier had been too close to call ended in a landslide victory for Socialist Party leader José Luis Rodríguez Zapatero. Incumbent president José María Aznar's defeat reflected widespread disgust with an executive that had lied about who the administration suspected was behind the tragic March 11 Madrid train station bombings that killed close to 200 people and wounded nearly 1,500. While Aznar publicly attempted to pin the blame for the bombings on the Basque terrorist organization ETA, it was clear to his administration that the leading suspects were Islamic extremists.

In addition, in spite of polls and massive demonstrations consistently showing that the vast majority of Spaniards opposed their country's participation in the Iraq invasion and occupation, Aznar allied with the US and committed Spanish troops. In the immediate wake of the 2004 Madrid bombings, Aznar knew Spaniards would interpret the attacks by Islamic terrorists as retaliation for what many Spaniards believed to be Spanish duplicity in an unjust war and occupation. Aznar's cover-up cost him the presidency. "We want the truth!" claimed thousands of Spaniards, and this cry, coupled with Zapatero's commitment to pull Spanish troops out of Iraq, handily won him the election.[37]

Zapatero's appeal to "the truth" comes at a moment when Spaniards are examining their pasts in unprecedented fashion. As Omar Encarnación argues, this examining of the past is catalyzed by several trends and events after an exceedingly long transition from authoritarian rule.[38] Perhaps most interestingly in relation to this book is the important and paradoxical Spanish role in the October 1998 London arrest of Chilean dictator Augusto Pinochet. Spanish magistrate Baltasar Garzón successfully filed an order for Pinochet's detention. After major wrangling among British, Chilean, and Spanish authorities, Pinochet's eighteen-month house arrest ended in his return to Chile rather than his extradition to Spain to stand trial for gross human rights violations. Yet there was no escaping the irony that a Spanish court was responsible for the arrest of Pinochet, for whom Franco served as an important role model.

Beginning in 2000, groups of Spanish citizens organized efforts to exhume the bodies of those killed during the 1936–39 Spanish Civil War and the repressive aftermath of the Franco regime. The Spanish parliament now actively debates how to characterize national dates that once stood as undisputed heroic moments. A new generation of Spanish academics is producing detailed studies of the Franco dictatorship, including the mass executions, the concentration camps, and the scope and range of repressive practices.[39] In what was once the exclusive domain of cultural production—film, fiction, art, theater—the grim past of the Franco regime has come alive, so to speak, in the Spanish body politic.

Nevertheless, there has been a limit to the reach of exploration. While the voiceless, the vanquished of the Spanish Civil War, have found some space for public expression, the silences continue regarding deep histories of conflict and violence embedded in the folds of the multiple constituencies of Spain and their relationships to "the national."

The spirits of the fifteenth- and sixteenth-century Spanish crusades that Franco resurrected and attempted to champion through several decades of the twentieth century were sentient in former president José María Aznar's rationale for his commitment of Spanish troops to the Iraqi invasion and in continuing Spanish troop commitments in Afghanistan and the region. In a speech delivered at Georgetown University, Aznar argued that Spanish engagement in Iraq must be placed in a specific historical context, and, in so doing, he offered an extreme Castillian version of Spanish relations with Islam:

> It is important to go back 1,300 years, to the beginning of the eighth century, when Spain was invaded by Moors and rejected being converted into one more piece of the Islamic world and began a long battle to recuperate her identity.[40]

Echoing this discourse, Spanish legislator and Popular Party spokesperson Gustavo de Aristegui asserted that Muslim resentment of Spain predated Spanish commitments in Iraq and Afghanistan by 500 years. In an editorial published in *The Washington Post*, Aristegui claimed that Islamic extremists had never accepted what he termed was the beginning of the end of Islam's Golden Age. The legislator argued that today, "like-minded democracies" must unite "at all costs" against what he described as a resentful enemy, a fallen people: "Now is the time for European societies to rally around the values and principles that have made our free countries the most stable, prosperous, and advanced nations on the planet."[41]

A video allegedly linked to the Islamist planners of the Madrid bombings evokes a haunting reminder of a distinct planetary status for Spain. The voice on the video claimed, "We all know about the Spanish crusades against the Muslims, the expulsions from Al Andalus and the tribunals of the inquisition."[42] The video resurrected the Spain of the Black Legend in relation to contemporary Spanish troop deployments in Iraq and Afghanistan, "the land of the Muslims." The voice on the video asserted that Spanish barbarity possessed deep roots.

What does it mean to resurrect the Crusades? For Castillian Spain, the Crusades evoke Christendom and empire, the Reconquest of territory from eight centuries of Islamic monarchic rule, the assertion of the end of Al Andalus. It signifies the expulsion and forced conversion of the Jews. It is the period of the unbridled conquest of the Americas. It is also a moment in which the Spanish empire controlled much of Europe. This mapping of European history is rarely resurrected outside Spanish history classes.[43]

There is comparatively little discussion of contemporary Spain's relationships to her pre-conquest, or pre-re-conquest, or "conquered" past, including the 800 years of Islamic rule over much of the country. Interestingly, the only monumental site more visited by foreign tourists than the *Valley of the Fallen* is the Alhambra castle of Granada, Spain, a spectacular Arabic complex encompassing a fortress (alcazaba), palaces (alcazares), and a small city (medina), constructed in the thirteenth century by the Nasrites. The Alhambra is a marvel of art, science, technology, light, plant life, air, water, and peace. The complex exudes Islamic contributions to art, religion, culture, and engineering that continue as weaves of the fabric of Spain.

In his major study *The Structure of Spanish History*, the renowned twentieth-century Spanish intellectual Américo Castro focuses primarily on the influences and traces of Jewish and Islamic traditions in what he termed a Spain of "many castes." Castro challenged Castillian versions of Spanish history that denied the deep influences of Islamic rule, as well as the impact of significant numbers of Muslims forced to convert to Christianity who remained in Spain before the ultimate mass expulsions in 1609:

> With those 900 years unfolded before our eyes, why should we find anything strange in the fact that the language, the customs, the religion, the art, the letters, and even the living structure itself of the Spaniard require, for understanding, that we bear in mind this interaction that continued for centuries? And we shall try to keep it in mind as something that gives a structure to history, rather than as the content of a national life. Let me repeat that Christian Spain was not something that preexisted in a fixed reality of her own, upon which fell the occasional influence of Islam, as a "mode" or a result of the life of "those times." Christian Spain "became"—emerged into being—as she incorporated and grafted into her living process what she was compelled to by her interaction with the Moslem world.[44]

In the wake of the March 11 bombings in Madrid and the revelations concerning the Islamic terrorists responsible, the *New York Times* offered this historical explanation of Islam in what is now Spain:

> For nearly 800 years, the Moors ruled Spain from its southern stronghold, El [sic] Andalus, ushering in a period of enlightenment and relative tolerance while the rest of Europe thrashed about in the Dark Ages. In 1492, the Spaniards reconquered the nation, forcing Muslims to convert, persecuting them and finally driving them back to where they came from.[45]

This is a peculiar, if unsurprising, mix of backhanded nodding to the Islamic dynasty's civilizing presence, coupled with the notion that there was some possibility of "return," after eight centuries, to "where they came from," as though after 800 years it was still an occupation, as if there were some neat division between Christians and Muslims that corresponded to territorial divides. As a Latin Americanist, I tried to imagine how such a notion would translate to the Americas, including whether one would attempt to claim that after three centuries of Spanish rule, the conquerors "went back to where they came from."

Just as there is little public discussion of Islamic–Christian encounter in the 800 years preceding the so-called reconquest, there is also little discussion of Spain's ongoing complicated relationship to North Africa. Tensions around the Spanish enclaves of Ceuta and Melilla emerge as periodic "irruptions" in an otherwise awkward and unspoken dimension of Spanish territoriality.[46] Ceuta and Melilla are home to approximately 140,000 Spaniards, often referred to as Christians, or Europeans, and roughly 40,000 Muslims, mainly from Morocco, who do not have full Spanish citizenship. Spaniards as a whole seem to wish these enclaves—remnants of the Spanish empire dating back to the fifteenth century, now inescapably carved as small chunks of territory from Morocco—would go away. Ceuta and Melilla were Franco's launch pads. They have become an integral part of "Fortress Europe," the *Valley of the Fallen*'s Army of Africa reincarnated.[47] The Spanish government maintains soldiers along a chain-linked fence and is in the process of constructing a $12 million wall in Melilla to guard against Africans attempting to cross the treacherous Straits to Europe. Meanwhile, Moroccans demand that Ceuta and Melilla be returned to Morocco. What does this staging suggest regarding Spain's constitutive features, as well as the fluidity of what are presented as starkly separate identities? In Spain, a country of forty-two million people, there are approximately one million Muslims, over half of whom are Moroccan.

Writer Juan Goytisolo stands as one of the most recognized living Spanish advocates of a public, dialogical exploration of the Islamic and Jewish constitutive elements of Spain. Deeply influenced by Américo Castro, Goytisolo confronts the foundational myths, exacerbated under the Franco regime, of a Christian Castillian Spain, at the expense of diverse regional, ethnic, and religious blendings, castes, and classes. Goytisolo's essays and fiction urge Spaniards to dismiss myths that he claims parallel Serbian, orthodox strands.[48] He warns that such myths exacerbate xenophobia and national and regional conflict.

Among the 200 who were killed in the March 11 bombings were approximately forty immigrants. Fouad Ait-Arouss, a restaurant employee, told reporters that when the attack occurred, "we all felt like Madrileños," citizens of Madrid.[49] On the first anniversary of the bombings, the Islamic Commission, a Muslim mediating body between the Spanish government and the country's Muslim community, issued a fatwa, a religious edict, condemning Osama bin Laden and Al Qaeda members as "apostates for their use of violence."[50] Most report that the backlash against the Muslim communities in Spain in the bombings' aftermath was mild. Yet in the years following the bombing, Madrid's leaders have seized the event to escalate its imperial strategy, and Spanish police have arrested well over 1,000 Muslims as terrorist suspects. Spain continues its strong alliance with Washington, including a major presence in Afghanistan.

Three weeks after the bombing, seven suspected leaders of the bombing died in an apparent suicide bomb explosion in a Madrid apartment. Starting mid-2007, twenty-eight defendants stood trial for the train bombings in a Spanish court, and in late October 2007, the court convicted twenty-one of them, including eighteen Moroccans and three Spaniards, to murder, forgery, and conspiracy to commit a terrorist attack.[51]

As a result of our visit to the *Valley of the Fallen*, Javier took up Father Laurentino's offer to spend several nights in the monastery in order to work on a film script. This was not an offer extended to me, as women are forbidden from spending a night in the monastery. Unbeknown to Father Laurentino, Javier was writing a script that questions a young girl's devotion to God on the eve of her death. The resulting movie, "Camino," which Javier also directed, won the Goya Award (Spain's equivalent of the Oscars) for best 2008 film but garnered tremendous wrath from the religious right, which is clearly affiliated with Laurentino and the Benedictine Abbey.

In any case, Javier spent three nights with the monks, attending masses, eating communal meals in silence, and exploring the crypt and its crevices. Needless to say, he got little writing done on his script. Instead, he took lots of photographs and wrote a detailed journal of his three days and nights in the *Valley*, not immune to several hauntings.[52] His journal was full of humorous as well as Edgar Allen Poe-like musings. The experience offered Javier a distinct lens on the *Valley*, among those who call it home.

It is clear that in the current debate regarding what to do with the *Valley of the Fallen*, the monastery and the Vatican consecration of the crypt as a Basilica complicate the picture. The 2007 Law of Historical Memory allowed for ceremonies at the *Valley of the Fallen* that are guided by "applicable norms with those generally characteristic of places of worship or public cemeteries."[53] In the Spanish senate legislation governing The *Valley of the Fallen*, passed in September 2010, the government is expected to convert the site into one that "honors and rehabilitates the memory of all those who fell as a consequence of the Civil War and the political repression that followed, with the objective of deepening knowledge of this historical period and consti-tutional values."[54] The conservative opposition Partido Popular voted against the legislation, claiming that the intent of the law is ultimately to do away with the Benedictine Abbey.

The *Valley*'s connection to Christendom and the Crusades parallels US presidential evocations regarding the country's "war on terrorism." While political analysts debated former president George W. Bush's intent when he referred in his September 16, 2001 speech to "this crusade" against "the

Figure 2.7 Detail of the *Albert Memorial*, depicting subjects of the British Empire
(photo by Katherine Hite).

evil-doers," few would refute the notion that Bush's discourse was theo-
cratically laced through and through. Indeed, scratch just below the Francoist
project surface and one will find uncanny analogies of heroes and martyrs,
good and evil, the West and the rest. The *Valley of the Fallen* represents a
provocative point of departure for global conversations that challenge these
oppositions, that acknowledge multiply constituted states and societies that
have emerged from deep histories of conflict and contact.

On my way home from Madrid, I visited a close friend, Jeanette Quinn,
in London. As I was on a monument kick, I had Jeanette take me around to
some of the more famous London monuments, including the recently restored,
shining monument commissioned by Queen Victoria to her beloved Prince
Albert. Guarding the steps of the monument are representations of the British
empire: statues meant to depict the African, Asian, and American colonies,
including an African tribesman with a lion, an elephant being patted by a
turbaned figure, and a native American. The four corners of the monument
lay claim to the gifts of the empire: commerce, manufacturing, engineering,
and agriculture. The monument lauds the great western philosophers, scientists,
and other intellectuals who have "bestowed" reason upon the globe. It is
remarkable in its pretensions and perhaps even more strongly than Franco's
monument, it projects the image of white imperial domination.

We then visited a small monument just off the River Thames, a few yards from the great London Eye. It is a monument to the 2,100 British citizens who, together with several thousand citizens from across the world, fought in the International Brigades to defend the Republic in the Spanish Civil War; 526 British men and women died in the war. The monument is a small, simple sculpture, and among the inscriptions on the plinth, one reads: "They went because their open eyes could see no other way." Jeanette and I talked about how to understand this inscription today—the idea of "open eyes," of international solidarity and individual sacrifice, of voluntarily giving oneself over completely to a social cause. In the chapters on Peru, Chile, and Argentina to follow, there are many who are memorialized who can clearly be described in the same ways.

The Brigadistas' participation in the Spanish Civil War represents yet another view into the globality of the war and the Francoist project. Jeanette and I also reflected on monumental contrasts. It is impossible to avoid thinking, as one stands before the International Brigades monument, about how many people walk by this statue each day without giving it even a glance. Such cannot be said for the *Valley of the Fallen*, nor for the Albert monument. Yet all monuments are open to interpretation, and their meanings change in relation to changing political moments and societal appropriations. As I stood before the International Brigade monument, I wondered who comes to commemorate those who fell.

3 Victims, victimizers, and the question of empathy

The Eye that Cries

In July 2007, I first walked *The Eye that Cries* memorial's labyrinthine path of smooth white stones. I arrived at the reflecting pool surrounding the great stone centerpiece Pachamama, Mother Earth, and I watched as the pool caught Pachamama's tears. A small fire had been lit, and smoke swirled around Pachamama like a soft mist. The sculptor Lika Mutal, who accompanied me to the space, sat quietly on the grass knoll bordering the memorial. I was deeply moved by the memorial's simple, exposed, peaceful space, and I remember thinking how odd it was that this memorial had become such a locus of editorial attack (and this was *before* the sculpture was, in fact, physically attacked).

The contrast between the aesthetics of *The Eye that Cries* and the grandiose, dark *Valley of the Fallen* memorial could not be starker. Spanish dictator Francisco Franco intended to remember those who died for church, crown, and country, a proclamation of victor's justice. The *Valley of the Fallen* projects statist, even imperial, power and force. As described in the previous chapter, inside the enormous crypt there are representations of centuries of colonialist domination exercised by both kings and papacies. By contrast, the Peruvian memorial evokes an ancient indigenous civilization, a fertility goddess mother, in mourning over great loss.

In spite of their dramatic differences, both the *Valley of the Fallen* and *The Eye that Cries* have stirred serious debates in their respective countries regarding how painful, violent pasts, both recent and not-so-recent, should be contemporarily understood and represented. Here we will examine Peruvian debates regarding how to understand and represent victims and perpetrators. In the case of *The Eye that Cries*, many Peruvians were outraged that specific dead individuals found a place in the memorial among the tens of thousands represented as victims. The anger laid bare the fraught politics of establishing a memorial to victims of a conflict when there are many layers and sites of conflict over time, and many who are implicated in and by terror. Judging who is a victim and who is not can constitute a complicated political as well as moral endeavor.

Beneath the tensions of casting victims and perpetrators in *The Eye that Cries* lies the similarly difficult but important question of the memorial's quest for empathy. *The Eye that Cries* exposes an uneasy politics in Peru regarding

Figure 3.1 Visitors to *The Eye that Cries*, Lima, Peru (photo by Gam Klutier).

the reaches and limits of understanding the trauma of "the other." From 1980–2000, the vast majority of those who lived in terror were indigenous peasants of the Peruvian highlands, physically and socially quite distanced from the dominant Peruvian metropolis of Lima. In many cases, violence emanating from both the military and *Sendero* destroyed collective organization, tore families apart, and left communities of widows and orphans. When individuals and families displaced by the violence in the Andes descended to Lima, they were often viewed with suspicion and fear. Drawing from both eastern and western philosophy and spirituality, *The Eye that Cries* seeks compassion for the descendants of those who are foundational to Peruvian identity yet who are structurally marginalized from power. This chapter asks how we might imagine the memorial evoking empathetic engagement, even in the context of frequent assaults on the sculpture. What are the limits to an empathetic politics, but what, too, are the possibilities?

Memorials not only represent distinct genealogies of trauma and violence, but also reflect and are part of ongoing struggle. The families whose loved ones are represented come to the memorial to mourn but also to demand justice. Fathers of university student activists, wives of union leaders, children of soup kitchen organizers, all grieve at the memorial but continue to evoke the memories of their loved ones' struggles for a just world, on university campuses, in union halls and neighborhood centers. The memories of their loved ones' politics are central to their struggle for accountability. If "memory" is indeed embedded in a memorial, then memory must be understood as a dynamic presence in the here and now.

Memorial conflicts

In November 2006, judges of the Costa Rica-based Inter-American Court of Human Rights issued a major ruling against the Peruvian government. The case centered on the 1992 military raid of Lima's high security Miguel Castro Castro penitentiary, an attack that took place under the Alberto Fujimori government (1990–2000). The attack targeted Cell Block 1A, housing close to 100 of the jail's female inmates. Peruvian military, police, and security forces sprayed the area with bullets, threw tear gas into the compound, and bombed and dynamited the cells. Over the course of four days, security personnel killed forty-one prisoners. Dozens of visiting family members were also subjected to the tear gas and bombings. Surviving former prisoners, including several women who were pregnant at the time of the attack, testified that they were brutally beaten and tortured.[1]

The Inter-American Court determined that the Peruvian government should pay the families of the dead prisoners and the tortured survivors approximately twenty million dollars in damages. The Court ordered the state to assume responsibility for the ongoing counseling many survivors sought for their traumatic experiences, as well as for the burial expenses and many legal, transportation, and other costs incurred by the families. And in an unusual move, the Court also specified that the Peruvian government should add the names of the forty-one dead to the approximately 32,000 Peruvians commemorated in *The Eye that Cries*, a Lima memorial to victims of the political violence that wracked the country through the late twentieth century.[2]

The dead prisoners were organizers and militants of *Sendero Luminoso*, or the Shining Path, Peru's notorious guerrilla movement. *Senderistas* waged armed conflict from the early 1980s until the mid-1990s. By then, the government had captured and jailed much of *Sendero's* top leadership. The conflict claimed almost 70,000 lives and destroyed and displaced entire communities. Both *Senderistas* and the army conducted massacres. Peru's 2003 official truth commission report estimated that the *Sendero* insurgents inflicted more than half the number of casualties.

Most Peruvians today consider those whom the government forces killed in Castro Castro to be terrorists responsible for ruthless killing and fear. As part of their assault on the Peruvian state throughout the 1980s and 1990s conflict, *Sendero* militants targeted popular local leaders and grassroots organizers who resisted their objectives. The insurgents used brutal tactics against a vast range of the citizenry. They tortured and executed their enemies in front of their children. *Senderistas* virtually enslaved remote indigenous communities in Peru's northern Amazon. Peruvian politicians charged that the Inter-American Court could not somehow equate the *Sendero* militants' deaths with those of tens of thousands of innocent victims, even if the government

Figure 3.2 Detail of the engraved stones along the labyrinthine path of El Ojo que
Llora (photo by Gam Klutier).

had violated human rights laws. To protest the ruling, Peruvian officials and
others, including the well-organized Association of Families of the Victims
of Terrorism, called for the Peruvian government to resign from the Court.[3]

Yet in an ironic twist, Peruvians would soon discover that among those
whose names were inscribed in *The Eye that Cries* memorial sculpture,
several, if not all, of the dead *Senderistas* were already represented there. The
sculptor intended the memorial to commemorate *all* the victims of the violence,
and she reproduced all the names from the lists of tens of thousands of deaths
and disappearances provided by the government truth commission. Dozens
of artists, human rights activists, religious, and others had collectively
participated in inscribing the names, dates, and years of births and deaths on
the stones that comprise the monument.

International human rights law defines those killed extra-judicially,
including convicted criminals, as victims. Until the Inter-American Court
ruling, the term, "victim," in relation to *The Eye that Cries* memorial, conveyed
a generic quality, a remote, passive, depoliticized character. The ruling lay
bare that the victims of the violence represented by the memorial included
combatants, sympathizers, and resisters, as well as men, women, and children
in a time of tremendous violence. Conscripted soldiers tortured, raped, and
killed and were killed. Indigenous youth as young as nine or ten both willingly
joined and were forcibly recruited into *Sendero Luminoso*. Communal civilian

patrols beat twelve-year-old *Sendero* suspects to death. The victims included those assassinated in extra-judicial killings while under arrest, those who had been formally charged as terrorists, as well as those awaiting sentencing.

The vast majority of Peruvians view the *Senderistas* killed in jail as terrorists. The revelation that the dead *Sendero* militants were inscribed at the site led to demands for the removal of the names, and among some sectors, for the demolition of the memorial altogether. Municipal authorities of Jesús María, the middle-class neighborhood in which the memorial stands, joined the call to remove the names.[4] Some members of the press dubbed the memorial, "The Monument to Terrorism."[5]

Human rights groups and prominent Peruvian cultural and political figures, including most visibly the Nobel laureate Mario Vargas Llosa, mobilized to defend *The Eye that Cries*. In an opinion editorial published in Spain's national daily *El País* and subsequently carried in newspapers throughout Latin America, Vargas Llosa argued that the memorial was a beautiful, arresting sculpture that powerfully evoked the suffering of all Peruvians who continue to struggle through painful reconciliation in the wake of the terrorism and violence. Moreover, as an ardent defender of private and intellectual property rights, Vargas Llosa argued that because the memorial was a private effort erected with private funds, only the sculptor herself should have control over the aesthetics of the memorial.[6] Vargas Llosa suggested that the sculptor consider turning over the stones of the Shining Path dead.[7]

Human rights activists and relatives of victims of the violence marched in defense of the memorial. They carried signs with calls for reconciliation, as

Figure 3.3 Mourning a loved one (photo by Gam Klutier).

Figure 3.4 A commemorative gathering (photo by Gam Klutier).

well as photographs of their dead and disappeared family members.[8] Marchers included peasants from Ayacucho, the center of the worst conflict and a former *Sendero* stronghold. Some of the peasant marchers had served several months in prison and had been recently released after the government exonerated them from charges they were terrorists.[9] For these many and varied defenders of the memorial, *The Eye that Cries* had assumed significant personal, moral, and political meaning.

The defenders of the memorial successfully staved off the call for demolition. Yet many months later, on the night of September 23, 2007, a group of men and women physically attacked *The Eye that Cries*. The group beat and tied up the municipal policeman guarding the memorial. The attackers smashed several of the stones, damaged the central stone representing Pachamama, and poured neon orange paint over Pachamama and segments of the stones that form the labyrinth. They left paint cans floating in the pool of water surrounding the central stone. This would be the first of several attacks on the memorial.

Situating the memorial in the political

The Castro Castro prison massacre occurred in May 1992, two years into the presidency of Alberto Fujimori (1990–2000) and a good ten years into the internal armed conflict and horrific brutality in the highlands. At that time,

Fujimori enjoyed considerable popularity. He assumed the presidential post in the wake of the disastrous first administration of Alan García (1985–90), who exited the country amidst hyperinflation, a failure to stem *Sendero's* violent ascendancy in Lima, systematic human rights violations by both the Peruvian security forces and *Sendero*, and the president's own corruption scandals.

Fujimori immediately instituted economic "shock therapy," a major contraction of state spending that triggered greater unemployment but succeeded in halting hyperinflation. In addition, he implemented dramatic internal security measures that formalized and "nationalized" the Peruvian security forces' right to detain and hold citizens virtually at will—practices that had already been in place since 1982 in the declared emergency zone of Ayacucho, where *Sendero* was born. In September 1992, four months after the Castro Castro raid, the military captured *Sendero* leader Abimael Guzmán and several top leaders. By the mid-1990s, Peruvian military and intelligence effectively ended Shining Path's attacks in Lima as well as the insurgency's general strength in the country.

In April 1992, one month before Castro Castro, Fujimori orchestrated an *auto-golpe*, an executive shutting down of the national congress. This move quashed congressional dissent in the face of Fujimori's economic and security reforms. The *auto-golpe* would later be condemned as the first major sign of Fujimori's "quasi-dictatorship," yet at the time a clear majority of the country supported the takeover. In 1995, Fujimori restored the congress and was overwhelmingly re-elected president.

While Fujimori remained popular through the end of the 1990s, it was also beginning to surface that Fujimori's power rested in good part on a vast network of spies, bribes, and blackmail. In May 2000, Fujimori won a third term amidst charges of vote-rigging and massive demonstrations against him. Shortly thereafter he fled to Japan, as news broke that Fujimori's chief intelligence officer Vladimiro Montecinos had videotaped himself paying bribes to an array of politicians and other government officials. The interim government began a series of investigations into Fujimori's administration. In addition, the government re-joined the Inter-American Court, heeded the recommendations of human rights organizations and proposed legislation establishing the Peruvian Truth and Reconciliation Commission (CVR). The CVR was charged with investigating the mass violence of the past two decades and the corruption of Fujimori's ten-year reign.

Dispositions toward Fujimori shifted markedly over the course of his presidency. At the time of Fujimori's ordering of the 1992 prison raid at Castro Castro, Fujimori could viably claim he had a popular mandate to take dramatic action to defeat the Shining Path guerrillas. *Sendero* had arrived in Lima. However, since the mid-1980s, newly established human rights organizations and associations of families of victims had publicly called attention to the systematic human rights violations against peasant highland communities —the deaths, disappearances, and massive displacements that devastated highland regions throughout the 1980s, initially conducted by the military, subsequently carried out by the Shining Path as well.[10] In small communities throughout the highlands areas worst affected by the violence, the devastation was (and continues to be) palpable. By the late 1980s in southeast Ayacucho, entire villages were composed chiefly of widows and orphans.[11] Yet despite the consistent efforts of human rights organizations to publicize and denounce the violence, it would take *Sendero Luminoso's* gaining major ground in Lima to force what had been invisible or denied to become visible and undeniable.

Sources estimate that at its height, *Sendero* possessed some 7,000 militants. Unlike other 1980s guerrilla movements in Latin America, *Sendero* could also claim that none of its financing or military support emanated from beyond Peruvian borders, a claim the Peruvian military acknowledged. *Sendero's* ability both to survive military attacks and to grow significantly over the 1980s raised important questions regarding the guerrilla movement's strategic capacity, the military tactics that not only failed to end *Sendero*, but also arguably contributed to *Sendero's* appeal, and the underlying historical–structural conditions that made a Maoist-inspired uprising against the Peruvian state not entirely surprising.

Nonetheless, most accounts portray *Sendero's* appeal in the countryside as temporary, as villagers grew wary of the guerrillas' directives and as communities were forced to endure the massive repression of the counterinsurgency. Based largely on previously existing forms of collective organization, communities formed *rondas campesinas*, or communal protection committees, to confront *Sendero*.[12] Some *rondas* were created under orders of the Peruvian military, while others were more autonomous. *Ronderos* engaged in armed clashes with *Sendero* and captured and executed *Senderistas* and *Sendero* suspects, both in their own communities and in neighboring ones. *Sendero* massacred entire families associated with the *ronderos*.

In their studies of communities in Ayacucho, Peru, the region in which confrontations between the military and the Shining Path most occurred, Ponciano del Pino and Kimberly Theidon reveal a pattern of narration in indigenous accountings of the recent past they have termed "toxic memory."[13] Toxic memory emerges from experiences of intense, direct violence within a community or between neighboring communities for which there is no recourse, no sense of the possibility of social justice, nor remorse from the perpetrators. Theidon emphasizes the complexity of the legacies of violence:

> The forms of violence suffered *and* practiced influence the reconstruction process when the fighting subsides. The fratricidal nature of Peru's internal armed conflict means that in any given community, ex-*Senderistas*, current sympathizers, widows, orphans, and veterans live side-by-side. This is a charged social landscape. It is a mixture of victims and perpetrators . . .[14]

Public memory debates in such settings are explicitly constrained by the knowledge of what violence particular agents are capable of exacting and by power dynamics that make no guarantees that such violence will be prevented in the future.

Nevertheless, over the past several years, difficult but distinct forms of what we might term an empathetic politics have taken place in the Andean highlands. Villagers have accepted—not without reluctance and suspicion, but they have accepted—the return of former *Sendero* combatants in exchange for ex-combatants' confessions, apologies, and in several cases, their communal work.[15] Here, empathy can be conceptualized as some understanding of an enemy, of how a fellow villager might become a *Senderista*. This understanding, in contexts in which "brothers" killed and were killed, allows for coexistence and the re-forging of social relationships. Empathy might also speak to what Theidon has called "the political economy of reconciliation," that is, the material, spiritual, and communal need for more fluid, socially contingent moral judgments regarding violence and its aftermath.[16]

Establishing the memorial

Fujimori fled the country in 2000. The interim government, led briefly by Valentín Paniagua (2000–01), took major steps to re-establish civil and political rights and the rule of law. Human rights groups were hopeful that a new moment had dawned, and the groups worked closely with the government for a series of measures to confront the abuses of the past twenty years and to seek redress for human rights victims. Several human rights leaders entered the new government.[17]

The CVR represented the major product of this collaboration between human rights groups and the governments of Paniagua and Alejandro Toledo (2001–06). It faced the formidable task of investigating a range of cases in which local and national elected politicians were implicated in repression and denial, and in which members of the indigenous communities collaborated in the killings. In addition, the CVR was charged not only with investigating the abuses during the major internal armed conflict (1980–93), but also with documenting President Fujimori's increasing abuse of power after militarily defeating the guerrilla movement (1993–2000).

Influenced in part by the South African Truth and Reconciliation Commission, the CVR conceptualized its mission as one of promoting reconciliation through extensive documentation and analysis of two decades of violent conflict; close attention to communities that had been the most directly affected by the conflict; nationally televised public hearings (though unlike the South African process, no one could be granted amnesty in exchange for truth-telling); and detailed recommendations of the institutional reforms deemed necessary to facilitate reconciliation and prevent future conflict. Peruvian and international anthropologists played key roles in communicating the CVR's mission to indigenous villages and in gathering testimonies. To demonstrate their commitment to investigating abuses in the highlands, truth commissioners bore witness to several mass exhumations.

The CVR produced a nine-volume report that locates the emergence of *Sendero* in the late 1970s within the historical–structural inequalities of the highlands, as well as within local political power dynamics and an evolving regional educational system that produced *Sendero*-affiliated teachers in particular highland communities.[18] The report addressed the range of perpetrators and facilitators of violence at the national, regional, and local levels, from state security forces to elected local and national officials, political parties, vigilante groups, and guerrillas—all implicated, according to the CVR, to one degree or another in the violence that had wrought the country.

Like many official truth commissions around the globe, the CVR recommended that as part of symbolic politics toward reconciliation, the government should sponsor memorials to commemorate the victims of the violence. Drawing in good part from this recommendation, human rights groups pressed for physical sites that would mourn the losses, publicize the past violations, and convey a strong message of "Never Again." Human rights groups envisioned an *Alameda de la Memoria*, a Walkway of Memory, as a site for contemplation and education.

The Eye that Cries memorial represented one seminal piece of a larger memorial project initiated by the Peruvian human rights community in conjunction with municipal authorities. Municipalities of Peru function as independent legal bodies whose authorities have jurisdiction over the use of public space. The mayor of the central Lima municipality of Jesús María from 2003 to 2007 maintained a close relationship with the major human rights organization *Asociación Pro Derechos Humanos* (APRODEH), whose offices are in the same municipality. Local authorities and civil society groups negotiated the *Alameda de la Memoria* as a tract within Jesús María's Campo de Marte, one of the major public parks of Lima. Architect Luis Longhi designed a landscape of pathways and green space that brings together distinct representations of memory within the *Alameda*. Families who lost loved ones in the conflict could find a space for mourning and reflection.

The internationally renowned sculptor of *The Eye that Cries* raised major funding from sources who were not known for their support for human rights initiatives. They included major Peruvian private conglomerates whose owners contributed money, engineering expertise, labor, and heavy machinery to excavate and prepare the site. When the controversy regarding the *Senderista* stones broke, the captains of industry were outraged that terrorists could be represented in the memorial. One well-known industrialist who had helped fund the memorial had himself been kidnapped and held for six months underground by Peruvian guerrillas.

Victims as well as perpetrators range the social spectrum, and the traumas are vivid as well as varied. As Cathy Caruth has suggested, there is an undeniable literality to many memories of traumatic experiences.[19] Rather than exorcising their traumatic experiences, survivors must often find ways of integrating these experiences into their identities.[20] Finding points of encounter that allow individual and collective, victim and viewer "working through" thus becomes a central challenge. This raises one of the essential dimensions of memorials: public recognition of the need for an environment in which to facilitate or contribute to an empathetic process. Representations of what took place must strive for empathy, even if what in fact occurs through representations is the exposure of profound difference. Empathy can be understood as a relation among human beings that may, in fact, question the distance between those who were held and those who could have been held, those who killed and those who could have killed.

The memorial's economic backers remained involved in the project, assured by the sculptor and intrigued by the memorial's representation of the violence. As Mario Vargas Llosa's support would attest, *The Eye that Cries* struck an aesthetic chord with the Peruvian elite, opening at least the possibility for unusual empathetic alliances across race and class.

The many meanings of *The Eye that Cries*

The creator of *The Eye that Cries* memorial is Lika Mutal, a Dutch-born sculptor who has lived in Peru for forty years. When she read statements in local newspapers that claimed her monument was "an homage to terrorists," Mutal felt she was facing "the most incredulous moment of [her] life."[21] Mutal wishes her memorial to be understood as a humanistic effort to awaken the consciences of all Peruvians to the violence and suffering of the recent past, as well as to encourage reflection regarding the relationships between painful memories and a more just, solidaristic Peru.[22]

Mutal roots her inspiration for the memorial in her visit to the 2003 exhibit, "Yuyanapaq: To Remember," a devastating, haunting display of 200 documentary photographs, organized by the Peruvian truth commission. The photographs provide a visual account of the gradual evolution of the conflict from the early 1980s through its escalation in the mid-1980s, to *Sendero*'s offensive in Lima that began in 1989. Several photographs capture the faces of families, despairing and uncertain, standing outside their destroyed homes. One photograph features a pair of small, weathered hands, cupped open to share a small portrait photo of a man. Other photographs show armed villagers. Another photo depicts captured *Sendero* militants training themselves in prison. One photo is of a group of men under arrest, seated in lines on the ground, with their heads bowed and their hands tied behind their backs. Like so many others who visited the exhibit, Mutal found herself both drawn into and intensely moved and saddened by the images of loss, mourning, conflict, and destruction.

After viewing "Yuyanapaq," Mutal returned to her studio and began to work through her own coming to terms with the enormity of the traumas represented. To center her piece, Mutal sculpted a representation of the ancestral goddess Pachamama. Mutal shaped Pachamama from an ancient, pre-Inca stone she had found on a trek in northern Peru years before, and in the stone she affixed another rock as an eye. A trickle of water runs continually from the rock, as

Figure 3.5 Sculptor Lika Mutal walking the labyrinthine path of stones (photo by Gam Klutier).

an eye that cries, that mourns the violence. The stone of Pachamama conveys a maternal quality of the familiarity and ongoing duress of suffering, implicitly against a notion of a masculine inflicting of violence. The representation also projects an eternal sense of victimization, neither periodizing nor romanticizing a "pre-violence" or "pre-conflict" historical moment. Mutal represents the genealogy of the victims as long and deep.

Encircling the stone is a labyrinthine path that consists of eleven thick bands of rock. Mutal drew the labyrinth concept from the thirteenth-century Chartres Cathedral labyrinth of France.[23] The Chartres labyrinth is meant to be walked from the outside to the center as a pilgrimage, to seek repentance, as a quest to become closer to God. For Mutal, the labyrinthine path is also a pilgrimage, in which visitors walk "in search of forgiveness, cleansing, and reconciliation within themselves and with others."[24]

In *The Eye that Cries*, 32,000 rocks, naturally worn smooth by seawater, form the bands of the labyrinth. Of these rocks, 27,000 carried the names, ages, and years of the deaths or disappearances of victims of the violence, all in alphabetical order. Approximately eighty artists, religious and spiritual activists and others participated in the initial inscribing process. Mutal recounted how she alone inscribed the name of a three-year-old girl on the last rock.[25] Visitors are meant to follow the rock path from outside in, contemplating the inscriptions, arriving ultimately at the center stone, face to face with the sorrow of Mother Earth.

In the two years following the inauguration of *The Eye that Cries*, the powerful rays of the sun erased the inscriptions. Groups of people came to re-inscribe sections of the rocks. Torn by the controversy, Mutal had to weigh, discuss, and debate in her own mind and heart and with others, how to treat those stones. She condemned the terrorism and the terrorists, uncomfortable with the idea of re-inscribing the names of the *Sendero* militants, haunted by the acts *Senderistas* committed. "Nature has taken care of their erasure here," she said.[26] Yet, aesthetically, philosophically, and spiritually, Mutal did not want the vast number of stones to remain whitened by the sun. "I want to remember and re-inscribe the innocent victims, and I cannot see how the terrorists can lie side by side with the innocents."[27]

How can one judge? If we explore what took place within Andean highland communities during the twenty-year conflict, we find that fabrics that had held these communities together unraveled, and that inter- and intra-village tensions and disputes that had been latent before the major conflict were manipulated in violent, destructive ways. Soldiers and civilians, combatants and non-combatants committed atrocities. Mutal described how a mother of a soldier who died in the conflict approached her to ask that Mutal inscribe a stone in his memory. While the soldier had received a military burial replete with honors and decorations for his service, the mother wished to have her son commemorated among the vast range of those who died, to be represented in a distinct individual and collective sense.[28] In this space, the mother can feel the son as a victim as well as a patriot. This fluidity might grant space for connection across difficult lines.

On the other hand, some who visit *The Eye that Cries* may very well read this mother's son as a perpetrator. Doris Caqui, whose husband was a labor leader taken away by security forces never to be seen again, claims that *The Eye that Cries* provides a space for her to mourn because there is no other space.[29] She knows that soldiers who killed as well as grassroots leaders who were killed share this space. "*The Eye that Cries* must be seen as a place that unites all the families without exception!" Mrs. Caqui says emphatically. "Victims are victims, and we are not in favor of excluding anyone."

Mr. Roca echoes this sentiment, and like Mrs. Caqui, he marched to defend the memorial. Mr. Roca's son, a university student activist, is also a *desaparecido*, abducted by security forces. "They say that we cannot have people who are terrorists here," said Mr. Roca, "but when the government killed them like that, they are *victims*, they are *victims*! It's as simple as that!"[30]

On April 27, 2007, Mr. Roca and Mrs. Caqui met me in the offices of APRODEH to share their accounts of their loved ones and to answer my questions. Midway through our interview, we turned to the subject of *The Eye that Cries*. "For those of us whose loved ones are *desaparecidos*, who do not even have the remains of our loved ones, this is the space where we come together to remember them, to place a candle, a photograph, a flower,"

Mrs. Caqui said. Until this point, Mrs. Caqui had been stoic, and her testimonial came at a rapid, forceful pace. Here, however, she broke down. "It is extremely important," she said, fighting to hold back her tears.

Mrs. Caqui and Mr. Roca talked about commemorative services and vigils in communities throughout the country. "We need other 'Eyes that Cry' in other parts of the country, so that many will become involved, as our 'Eye that Cries' has invited people here to become involved, to think and re-think our memories," Mrs. Caqui said. (And indeed, as illustrated in Figure 3.6, communities in the remote Andean highlands have reproduced Mutal's design, creating "little eyes," as they have been termed.) When we finished the interview, Mutal was waiting to accompany me to *The Eye that Cries*. Mr. Roca approached Mutal, and with tears in his eyes, he quietly implored her to re-inscribe his son's name on the stone.

As *The Eye that Cries* tensions illustrate, traumas and the memories of politics must be spoken; they cannot be avoided if we are to imagine a pluralized or democratized politics. Traumas can be represented, voiced, and acknowledged. This does not necessarily mean reconciliation will follow. But there must be space for voice, many voices. Often, ordinary citizens confront the state and one another, forcing the state to negotiate representations and creating unanticipated meanings that capture something of the pain of the trauma, the trace. As in rituals echoed at memorials around the world, families from many walks of life come to *The Eye that Cries* to locate the stones that represent their loved ones, and they often leave flowers and other mementos of remembrance.

Mrs. Caqui and Mr. Roca made *The Eye that Cries* a memorial of their own. This can represent a distinct kind of tension between the memorial maker and those who come to find solace in the memorial and, ultimately, to claim it. Sometimes, and often in small ways, people can interact with one another at traumatic memory sites, to try to understand or contextualize the atrocities in order to imagine a different humanity.[31] Mrs. Caqui described the dialogue that has begun between herself and other families of the disappeared, on the one hand, and the parents of Mariela Barreto, an intelligence agent implicated in several kidnappings, including that of Mr. Roca's son, on the other. Barreto's name is inscribed on a stone at *The Eye that Cries*.

Memorials thus can invite a tremendous range of engagement, from the intimately private identification with the representation that may emanate from victims and their families, to the less direct, less intense but nonetheless evocative, contemplative response a memorial might catalyze for a host of publics. As my own experience of visiting the memorial can attest, *The Eye that Cries* is deeply moving to many visitors who are not direct victims of the violence.[32] Mutal expressed the wish that visitors think, feel, and experience the memorial.[33] She hopes that they experience how "everything becomes now, just consciousness."[34] For Mutal, who is influenced in part by Buddhist teachings, accepting that the violence has occurred underlines the need for compassion in the present.

Figure 3.6 El Ojo que Llora of Llinque, Peru (photo from Archivos APRODEH).

The beauty and power of Mutal's memorial also lies in its abstraction. In the twenty-first century, societies are inundated, even overwhelmed by graphic violent imagery, at home and around the globe. When confronted with violent, representational art, viewers may instinctively turn away from, reject, feel a numbness, as if viewers are being forced to be reminded once again that there is a great deal of violence in the world, a phenomenon they already know and don't need or want to contemplate. Mutal's visual representation of *The Eye that Cries* steers clear of "literal memory," which may have the unintended consequence of insulating the victims, as viewers shun the representations.[35] Abstract commemorative art is that which moves viewers to react, but perhaps in a less immediate, more contemplative way that recognizes their distance, that acknowledges that viewers can connect and feel even when they cannot really know what it was to experience such trauma.

Scholars such as art historian Jill Bennett argue that memorial art that is too representative of a violent trauma, art that is too representational, too graphically violent, risks laying a false claim to an experience "owned" by others.[36] Bennett argues that the art of trauma has to find an in-between, respecting the profound trauma of victims' experiences while appealing to the senses and sensibilities of those who were not the victims. Through artistic representations of trauma, Bennett is seeking "empathy not grounded in affinity (feeling for another insofar as we can imagine being that other) but on a feeling for another that entails an encounter with something irreducible and different, often inaccessible."[37] Bennett searches for art that evokes *empathic unsettlement*, that is, "to describe the aesthetic experience of simultaneously *feeling for* another and becoming aware of a distinction between one's own perceptions and the experience of the other."[38] In a similar vein, Geoffrey Hartman, creator of the Holocaust testimonial collection at Yale University, warns that sympathy is an indispensable response but one that must be checked: "Art expands the sympathetic imagination while teaching us about the limits of sympathy."[39] Pity, the "feeling sorry for" that characterizes sympathy, may foreclose our reach toward empathy, the more profound "feeling with" another's pain.

Memorializing is a conjunction of affect and awareness. Mutal can compassionately exclaim through Pachamama's eye that Mother Earth feels the horrendous violence and, therefore, she cries. The artist invites viewers to connect their own losses and sorrows with those of Pachamama. For Mutal herself, the act of sculpting Pachamama brought back memories of the traumatic experience of coming face to face with violence and death as a young child in Holland during World War II. She remembered a boy being pushed by a German soldier into a truck and taken away. She remembered another boy running for his life, shot, and lying in the snow. "I realized," Mutal said, "that *The Eye that Cries* was in part my search for personal redemption of my human condition."[40]

The politics of perpetrators, victims and trauma time

As *The Eye that Cries* demonstrates, the impact and intensity with which both the makers and the publics engage memorials can refuse neat chronologies through time. As a memorial site, *The Eye that Cries* initially received few visitors—human rights activists, families of victims, an occasional school group, and foreign tourists. The Inter-American Court decision brought unanticipated attention to the sculpture, and *The Eye that Cries* has now become a far more visible site of contestation.

Memorials have the potential to symbolize and enact traumas that suspend and transcend temporal conventions. Trauma time extends backwards and forwards independent of the moment. Mutal's representation of Pachamama locates time in an ancient and seemingly eternal place that is also very present, among the indigenous majority of Peru. Pachamama is like an historical conscience, an inescapable, powerful grounding force in trauma time. International relations scholar Jenny Edkins argues that trauma time challenges linear time, and that memorials may expose the disjuncture between an official temporal account and lived experiences. This also raises the question, how do we know when we are no longer in trauma time?

Memorials cannot impose closure—a "post" to conflict. *The Eye that Cries* mourns a deep, painful past. While the mass killings have stopped, the killings themselves are all too recent, and in my 2007 visit to Ayacucho, Peru, the region most affected, the fear and distrust generated from the two decades of conflict were quite palpable. For the women of Ayacucho's Association of Families of Kidnapped, Detained, and Disappeared of Peru (ANFASEP), the fact that the same man, Alan García, who was president of Peru during the period of their loved ones' disappearances, was back in the presidency, contributed to this fear and distrust. One member of ANFASEP told me that seeing García's face on a television screen or in a newspaper was like "reliving a nightmare."[41] How, then, should governments address the issue of those who were brutalized is enormously complicated.

In the discourse about victims of political violence, there is often a denial of agency or resistance rather than a recognition and respect for the fact that the brutalized were also social, political human beings. It is like characterizing activists as tsunami victims. In the Peruvian highlands, local and regional indigenous communities organized self-defense committees—at times in collaboration with state security forces, but not always—who fought the Shining Path and killed suspected *Sendero* militants and collaborators. Other indigenous individuals, families and groups joined the Shining Path. Victims, perpetrators, resisters, and survivors come from many sides of the conflict and can often be read as all of the above and more.

The process of establishing a memorial's design can also involve political co-optation. Recently, in countries such as Argentina and Chile, for example, the political leadership has come to recognize that past traumas must be incorporated or integrated into a national identity that neither denies nor represses the trauma. For better and for worse, politicians across the spectrum have come to accept the inevitability of the continued unearthing of traumatic pasts, and they view it as instrumentally strategic to take the offensive when it comes to symbolic representations of those pasts.

In an ongoing attempt to defend and bolster himself and curry favor with the Peruvian military and pro-Fujimori politicians, Peruvian president Alan Garcia (2006–11) continued to resurrect the all-too-recent memory of the militarily defeated Shining Path as a haunting presence and ongoing threat. During his first term in office (1985–90), García gave the military virtually unchecked authority to wage a counterinsurgency campaign against *Sendero*. In a rather miraculous comeback from his presidential record of gross economic and security mismanagement and corruption, García returned to the country after several years to reclaim his party's mantel and, ultimately, the presidency. He asserted that to hold the armed forces accountable for their counterinsurgency tactics "plays into the hands" of the Shining Path.[42] García charged that *Sendero* might have been "militarily but not politically defeated and therefore looks for ruses to present itself as a victim."[43] This assertion exacerbates the anxieties that are clearly felt in many of the indigenous communities most hit by the violence of the 1980s.

Both Peruvian human rights groups and the Inter-American Court continue to press that García himself be held accountable for massive abuses under his stewardship, including the deaths of 118 inmates during a 1986 military action to re-assume authority after a prison revolt at *El Frontón* prison. While the ex-commander in chief of the armed forces testified that he received orders from García to attack the prison, the president has yet to be prosecuted. Ayacucho special prosecutor Cristina Olazábal sought prosecution of García for the assassination of sixty-nine peasants in Accomarca, but Olazábal was accused of political motives for seeking the former president's prosecution and she was removed.

In November 2005, Chilean authorities surprised Alberto Fujimori. The former president arrived in Chile after five years of exile in Japan, whose government had refused to heed Peru's request for Fujimori's extradition. Fujimori seemed confident that the same would be true in Chile, a country not known for extraditing former heads of state. Imagining Chile as a strategic launch pad of sorts, Fujimori had hoped to stage a political comeback in Peru, where his daughter Keiko had become a popular politician and his political movement had regained strength. The arrest clearly caught Fujimori off guard. Several months later, the Chileans released Fujimori from arrest but ordered that he remain in the country pending the extradition hearings.

On September 21, 2007, after almost two years of judicial proceedings and deliberation, the Chilean Supreme Court ruled that Alberto Fujimori be extradited to Peru to face criminal human rights and corruption charges. The next day, Chilean police promptly returned Fujimori to Lima. The human rights community celebrated the Chilean court's extradition decision as an internationally precedent-setting human rights victory. The following night came the first physical attack on *The Eye that Cries* sculpture.

While no group claimed responsibility, most suspected this was the work of Fujimori supporters angered by their leader's arrest. Neon orange is the color of Fujmori's political movement. Most major media and several politicians, including Keiko Fujimori, publicly denounced the violent attack on the memorial. Yet some Fujimori supporters, including former presidential candidate Martha Chávez, applauded the attack, calling the memorial "garbage." "If civic leaders and defenders of the human rights of terrorists want to place victims and victimizers together, then let them make their monuments to terrorists in their offices, but they cannot use a public park."[44]

Lika Mutal, who had been out of the country until the evening of the attack, was clearly stunned by the brutality. The attackers used a heavy hammer to attempt to destroy the eye of the central stone. Mutal felt they took "special care to cover the names of the children [with the paint], the first stones that had been recently permanently engraved rather than handwritten."[45] Several days after the attack, APRODEH organizers, former Peruvian Truth Commission head Salomón Lerner, family members such as Mr. Roca and Mrs. Caqui, Lika Mutal and others marched to defend human rights, denounce the attack, and demand a full investigation.

The Eye that Cries once again returned to the public as a site of contestation, this time defended by a range of sectors that do not agree on who should be recognized as a victim, who a perpetrator, but who nonetheless hold the memorial as a beautiful, meaningful site of remembrance.

There have been several attacks on the memorial, a raw testament to the tensions between the Peruvian state and the Inter-American Court, as well as within the Peruvian state and society regarding the politics of memory and representation. The debates and the attacks focus on who constitutes a victim and who a victimizer, as well as who is a hero, who a terrorist.[46] Given such visible manifestations of tension, even rage, it might be naïve to urge imagining an empathetic politics derived from this memorial space.

Yet there are signs that the memorial has invited connection and solidarity across difference, and that the attacks served to enunciate as well as denigrate *The Eye that Cries*. In her analysis of the defacing of *The Eye that Cries*, historian Cynthia Milton underlines that the violent attacks do not silence but rather "provoke debate, dialogue and remembering."[47]

Before Mutal secured funding to re-inscribe the names through permanent machine engravings, APRODEH human rights advocate Rosario Narváez organized groups to come to *The Eye that Cries* to re-inscribe names manually. "Senior citizens are the best," Narváez recalls, "but so, too, are the young people, or people who come in from the provinces to re-inscribe the names on the stones."[48] "We re-inscribe silently, and we find ourselves wondering, 'Who was this person, who died in such-and-such-a-year?' It's hard work but it's cathartic at the same time, claiming this space, mainly writing in silence."[49]

In October 2010, Lima university students joined family members of the disappeared at *The Eye that Cries* to contribute to an ambitious knitting project, the creation of a great *"Chalina de la Esperanza,"* a "Scarf of Hope." The idea of a *chalina* was the inspiration of young women from Lima who wished to communicate their solidarity with the indigenous women who had lost their loved ones. When working with the Peruvian forensic anthropology team (EPAF) in the Andean highlands, the young women observed how the indigenous women identified the exhumed remains by rubbing tiny bits of cloth together—clothing that was more often than not sewn, knitted, and stitched by the indigenous women themselves.[50]

Like the rocks of *The Eye that Cries*, patches of the *chalina* bear the names and dates of the *desaparecidos*, and the collective *chalina*-making has taken place in various parts of the country. Each patch is different, and the bright colors of the yarns and cloth belie the underlying loss and pain. The young women of Lima, including Morgana Vargas Llosa, Mario Vargas Llosa's daughter, work with the indigenous women of the Andes, and like the senior citizens and young people of the provinces who once etched names into the rocks of *The Eye that Cries*, they wonder about who it is they remember. Such cultural processes and productions are forms of empathic unsettlement.

In spite of the fact that to be able to enter the memorial requires making an appointment and being accompanied by someone from APRODEH or by the sculptor herself, thousands have now visited the site.[51] In May of 2009, I attended a Mother's Day ceremony at *The Eye that Cries*. Approximately one hundred women and their families gathered, clustered on the grassy hill next to the memorial. There were many indigenous as well as *mestiza* women, and occasionally a family headed somberly to the memorial to walk the labyrinth, their heads bowed toward the stones. A daughter of a *desaparecido* recited a poem she wrote. A priest led the gathering in prayer. A small musical group played. It was clear that *The Eye that Cries* had become a place of collective, familial mourning and remembrance.

As moving translations of *The Eye that Cries*, several Peruvian highland villages have established *"ojitos,"* or "little eyes," memorials in their communities, at cemeteries and plazas, and the community of Llinque, Apurimac, created a somewhat smaller replica of *The Eye that Cries* for its central square.[52] Thus, just as tension marks *The Eye that Cries*, so, too, does the embrace.

In the aftermath of the attack, Mutal offered these reflections:

> Being in front of the big stone now vandalized and mutilated, one is struck by an even stronger expression of horror than the photographs of the vandalism can convey. It looks, moreover, like Pachamama is crying blood, and this calls for reflection. This wound—impossible to restore—represents the wound that in Peru throughout its history was never healed and that during the years of terrorism represents the wound we humans inflict upon life and upon each other since the beginning of our existence.

Looking into the eye of the Mother, which I must admit exudes a lethal beauty I become aware that—especially through personal introspection— we could and must transform this into the opposite, admitting the splendor of the creation as central to our existence and activating the gift of creativity and generosity with each other and ourselves, which life—also through us humans—offers us. If not, for what will we have lived?[53]

4 Searching and the inter-generational transmission of grief in Paine, Chile

"Did you hear?" twenty-one-year-old Gabriela Ortiz asked me as we sat down for coffee in July 2009. The remains of as many as nine of the seventy disappeared and executed men of Paine, Chile, had been discovered in a lakeside area a few miles south of town. The Paine families were fairly certain that the remains belonged to some of the men who on October 16, 1973, were rounded up from three different Paine peasant cooperatives. Now, thirty-five years later, there was a good chance that at least a few of the many men from Paine rounded up on that day alone would be positively identified and properly buried.

As a granddaughter of a Paine peasant leader murdered by the military in 1973, Gabriela was cautiously optimistic and upbeat about the Paine families' news, though she wasn't holding her breath. Many years earlier, in 1994, Chile's Medical Legal Service, the chief state forensic agency, claimed to be returning the remains of Luis Gaete, a twenty-one-year-old Paine farm worker.[1] His wife Rosa Becerra was heavily pregnant when Chilean army lieutenant Osvaldo Magaña and his men took Gaete away, and she would deliver their only child three weeks after his disappearance. Yet the remains that Rosa Becerra buried in 1994 proved not to be those of her husband Luis Gaete. In 2004, the government revealed that the Medical Legal Service had committed embarrassing, even shocking, misidentifications, including misidentifying several Paine family members. To this day Becerra does not know who she interred as Luis Gaete, whose grave she visited for ten years.[2]

In another instance, in 2001, in their first report to admit to institutional wrongdoing, the Chilean military included the name of Andrés Pereira, a Paine businessman and the father of well-known human rights lawyer Pamela Pereira, as one of the 200 victims they had executed. The report claimed that Pereira "was taken from his home on October 15, 1973, and that same day his body was thrown into the sea, off [the small coastal town of] Pichilemu."[3] Yet the Pereira family knew that the military's account did not add up. In June 2010, a year after my coffee with Gabi Ortiz and a good ten years since the military's deliberate misinformation concerning the whereabouts of Andrés Pereira, the results of DNA testing done by a laboratory in Austria finally confirmed the remains of the nine executed men.[4] Among the nine are Rosa

Becerra's husband, Luis Gaete, his brother Carlos, and Pamela Pereira's father, Andrés Pereira.

Gabi's own extended family's search for their loved ones was comparatively short-lived. The grandfather Gabi never knew, Luis Celerino Ortiz Acevedo, 36, and his brother Juan Manuel Ortiz Acevedo, 38, were both tenant farmers who had become leaders of the Rangue cooperative of Paine. Together with three other farm workers from Paine's nearby El Patagual cooperative, the five were arrested on October 13, 1973, and taken to the San Bernardo Infantry Regiment, the launching ground for virtually all Paine disappearances and executions. After being held for a week, the five men were executed. Two months later, their bodies were found at another Paine cooperative, Lo Arcaya. In November 1973, the Medical Legal Service officially informed the Ortiz families that the two brothers died from fatal bullet wounds.[5]

Until the mid-twentieth century, Paine, some thirty miles from Santiago, was a rural area constituted by large haciendas, a local aristocracy, and many tenant farmers and their families. From the mid-1960s to 1973, Paine became the site of major agrarian reform, including peasant struggles to establish cooperatives carved from the haciendas. The September 11, 1973, military coup led to the swift, concerted, and deadly retaliation against Paine's leading peasant organizers and their supporters. The sudden attack was supported by those who collaborated with security forces to identify and eliminate local peasant leaders and other activists. Collaborators and families of the victims co-exist in Paine today.

For the majority of the families of the victims of Paine, it has taken decades to clarify the fates of their loved ones, and some still wait. Like many families in Chile, the families of the disappeared and executed of Paine have undergone long, laborious, costly, unbelievably frustrating, heartbreaking journeys, through police precincts, detention centers, state ministries, politicians' offices, law firms, courts, morgues, and unmarked grave sites. And while many of the Paine families' loved ones have now been unearthed, and some of the perpetrators have been prosecuted, the searching for a deeper sense of meaning has not been resolved. Today's third generation seeks inspiration from their grandfathers' struggle for social justice. In this context of conflict, loss, and pain, the relatives of the disappeared and murdered of Paine have produced an uplifting, brightly colored, beautiful memorial of great historical importance.

A thousand pine logs, minus seventy, stand tall in the *Paine Memorial*. In place of the missing logs are family-designed mosaics filled with icons, from tractors, watermelons, and hoes, to guitars, and soccer balls. There are also political icons signaling political party militancy. And there are several mosaics with images of a mother crying, or outstretched hands. Recently, the grandchildren of Paine have placed plaques with their own messages on the mosaics.

To understand the juxtaposition of these many memorial symbols, we must closely explore and untangle the intense politics and history of three generations of Paine families. In essence, the *Paine Memorial* grew out of both an awakening consciousness and an increasing unraveling of denial. The memorial is an expression of mourning, and the symbols are interwoven with profound grief. Yet the memorial also powerfully expresses a living memory, insisted upon by the third-generation descendants of those who struggled. The grandchildren emphasize their desire to retrieve the humanity and inspiration of their grandfathers.

The *Paine Memorial* has become part of an international coalition of sites, and representatives from Paine regularly participate in meetings with other Latin American and international site representatives. Thus, on the one hand, Paine tells a very local story; yet Paine, too, forms part of a global imaginary.

Generations and postmemory

How does one approach a history that involves three different generations? For those who study political generations, there is a rough division into two major theoretical perspectives. The first view emphasizes social location, the coming of age in a particular historical–political moment. Sociologist Karl Mannheim, the most cited scholar on the latter, phenomenological approach to generations, argues that generations come into being when "similarly 'located' contemporaries participate in a common destiny and in the ideas and concepts which are . . . bound up with its unfolding."[6]

Quick scrutiny of members of particular generations reveals enormous political differences within them, yet terms such as the "Sixties generation" carry discernible connotations. Here, what distinguishes generations is their association, usually as young adults, with a dramatic, and often traumatic, event or series of events, such as the Great Depression, World War II, or for the US 1960s generation, the civil rights and anti-Vietnam war movements. Mannheim suggests that "generational units" form around "an identity of responses, a certain affinity in the way in which all move and are formed by their common experiences." Such units account for political–ideological conflict, as members of the same generation formulate distinct ideational responses to similar social conditions.

There are also those who concentrate on biology and the life course (i.e., adolescence, marriage, parenting) as central to an individual's political perspectives. For students of the Holocaust, the central question in generational studies is what is passed on within and across family members who are Holocaust victims. For example, scholars explore the effects of memories of the Holocaust on children who were born during the Holocaust but were too young to understand what was happening to them and around them. Holocaust literature addresses the ways in which youth lose family members and their childhood altogether, as well as children and grandchildren of Holocaust survivors who were born after the Holocaust but who grew up with the strong sense that they directly experienced the genocide of their elders.[7] Here, generations are defined by the trauma of the genocide and by the families who have borne trauma and who transmit, both consciously and unconsciously, their experiences to their children and grandchildren. The study of Chile and the *Paine Memorial* make both these generational approaches valuable.

Those whose lives are poignantly memorialized in the *Memorial of Paine* were primarily agricultural workers who participated in struggles to redistribute land and who lost. The families have attempted to work through the memories of their loved ones in the context of the lingering devastation of struggle and defeat. September 11, 1973 marks a clear before and after, as the disappearances and subsequent murders occurred in the two months immediately following the coup. Closely following, the military dictatorship carried out further arrests, ushering in dramatic structural changes, eliminating collectivities and the very concept of a social welfare state. The mothers, widows, children, and grandchildren of Paine thus search for meaning in a social, cultural, and political milieu that violently crushed the efforts of the peasants of Paine to equalize land distribution.

Paine, time, and trauma

Chile at mid-twentieth century was a country with a strong political party system, representing sectors across the ideological spectrum. Parties from left to right fielded national candidates. Centrist parties tended to ally alternately with the left or right to carry the presidential election.[8] Since the early 1900s, the historic left Communist and Socialist parties were more or less represented in both the executive and legislature, and their elected leadership came from Chile's cities and from the mining regions. In the Chilean countryside, the right maintained a political stronghold.

The lion's share of Chile's economic growth and stability came from Chile's mines, which in the 1950s and 1960s were predominantly owned by the United States. Tax revenues from the mines fueled public sector expansion and industrialization, and by the late 1960s, Chile's population was largely concentrated in urban areas. The agrarian sector remained underproductive, with vast, fallow farmland concentrated in a few family hands.[9] While politics in the cities were progressive, politics, society, and culture in the Chilean countryside were notably patriarchal.

This pronounced urban–rural divide was rooted in a political compromise that protected the Chilean ruling class. It was a kind of gentlemen's agreement by the Chilean left not to organize in the countryside in order, in good part, to ensure that the political right maintained its base of support for a national electoral presence and, inherently, a particular way of life.[10] Moreover, the stifling of left political organizing in the countryside was backed by laws that prohibited rural unionization and that failed to protect the rural secret ballot.

Beginning in the 1960s, this compromise would change. During the rightist government of Arturo Alessandri in 1962, Chile passed the nation's first agrarian reform law, pushed hard, interestingly, by the US, in order to model a Latin American antidote to the 1959 Cuban Revolution.[11] The 1962 legislation lacked both the political will and the necessary resources for implementation, but the door was now ajar. Subsequently, the Christian Democratic government of Eduardo Frei (1964–70), whose electoral victory was supported by the right, passed laws ensuring a secret ballot and legalizing rural organizing. In 1967, the Chilean landowning class first experienced under Frei what to this day would become its most resonant traumatic collective memory: expropriation.

For the Chilean economic elite, the 1960s were a nightmare, as new political parties professed revolutionary struggle, Christian liberation theologians, priests, and laypeople preached a preferential option for the poor, and the traditional communist and socialist left gained greater ascendancy.[12] Radicalization in the 1960s was certainly not unique to Chile, but the country's marked swing to the left at the height of the Cold War became a central cause for alarm, both for Chile's ruling class and for the United States. The extreme right in Chile began to mobilize major anti-communist campaigns and in 1970 formed the Nationalist Fatherland and Liberty movement, which included a paramilitary arm. US covert operations to undermine the Chilean left got well underway, and US Alliance for Progress assistance included military and police training in interrogation and the use of force against domestic targets.[13]

President Frei's betrayal led the political right in 1970 to field its own presidential candidate rather than throw its weight once more behind the centrist Christian Democrats. The left-wing Popular Unity coalition candidate, Socialist party leader Salvador Allende, narrowly won the three-way 1970 presidential race, and his government accelerated the agrarian reform process. Allende's victory propelled old and new left political party militants and sectors at the grassroots to organize and push for full implementation of the reforms, as well as to establish new political footholds in communities that had experienced little in the way of progressive politics.

In an impressive analysis of history and memories of violence and state terrorism in Paine for his undergraduate thesis, Juan René Maureira, who grew up in Paine and whose grandfather is a *desaparecido* of Paine, captures with both sensitivity and nuance the kinds of changes in Paine's social structure.[14] One of Maureira's central questions is why the violence of 1973 struck with such dramatic force in Paine? Why were more citizens per capita detained–disappeared and executed in Paine than in anywhere else in Chile?

To answer this, Maureira attempts to reconstruct the social climate in Paine in the years leading to the coup. He emphasizes the cultural and political significance of landholding for the Chilean elite, as well as the ways various forms of cultural and economic subordination threaded through Paine's agricultural working families. Maureira finds that until the mid-1960s, Paine was in many ways a classic mix of conviviality, gentility, paternalism, inequality, and hierarchy in a small town and rural community. With the agrarian reform movement, this mix was broken by the creation of new peasant cooperatives on what were large landholdings, growing from agrarian workers' new sense of the possible.

From this sense of the possible emerged an explosion of left-wing movements and action. This included young and not-so-young militants from the Socialist Party, the new left break-off from the Christian Democratic Party, the MAPU, and a newly formed revolutionary left MIR—all organized alongside their families and non-militant farm workers of Paine to establish cooperatives and widespread networks of support.[15] Among the organizers were the grandparents of Gabriela Ortiz and Juan René Maureira.

"My grandfather and his brothers were known as the wild ones, the radical ones of Rangue," Gabi said, laughing. "The Ortíz family is enormous, and our family name is like a label, we have a reputation."[16] For more than a century, Rangue and several neighboring Paine haciendas had been owned by the Letelier family and its descendants, whose vast wealth came from mining. Gabi's grandfather and three of her great-uncles participated actively in the 1971 *toma*, the takeover of the Rangue hacienda, which became a model Paine peasant cooperative.[17]

Others sympathetic to the *inquilinos'* struggle, such as Juan René's grandfather, René Maureira Gajardo, came to Paine in the 1960s—in René's case, from a sparsely populated province south of Paine. René Maureira and his wife Sonia Carreño Saldías established a small grocery store in town. As conflict over the redistribution of land and power intensified in Paine, René, a Socialist Party militant, was the only grocer in the area who kept his store stocked and accepted the government-imposed price freezes. Other Paine business owners deeply resented Maureira and accused him of betraying his own class interests.[18]

For one year after the *toma* of the Rangue hacienda, between September 1971 and September 1972, the Rangue cooperative ran exceedingly well. The approximately seventy tenant farmers who had once been contracted by the hacienda joined together to elect leaders and organize an effective division of labor, including committees to petition the government for formal–legal recognition and to determine what to grow and how. With some government technical support, the former *inquilinos* re-seeded land that had lay fallow for years, and the cooperative produced corn, wheat, and potatoes, as well as its traditional revenue base, grapes for wine. Once it gained legal recognition in early 1972, the cooperative used a government loan to purchase heifers imported from Uruguay and to establish a productive cattle business.[19]

Yet what happened in Paine ultimately could not be separated from conflicts that were growing day by day across the country. These conflicts took place not only between the right and left, but also within radical left parties and coalitions. By October 1972 and into 1973, the national conflicts sharpened the already tense relations in the several Paine cooperatives. For example, the CIA precipitated two long truckers' strikes that crippled Paine's produce transportation and exacerbated the shortage of goods. Rangue cooperative workers argued over the pace of change, including how, whether, or when to transform the cooperative into small privately owned parcels. The Rangue workers elected Gabi's great-uncle, Juan Manuel Ortiz, affiliated with the more radical MAPU, to be the new president of the cooperative. Gabi's grandfather Luis became head of the basic goods distribution program, which called itself the JAP. Women in the Ortíz family helped organize communal soup kitchens. Juan René Maureira's grandfather René also became a leader of the JAP, serving as a vital support link between the town and the cooperatives.

The once tranquil climate of Paine gave way to open tension and conflict, as the six Letelier sons alternated between stonewalling their former tenant farmers and negotiating with the government for compensation for their expropriated lands. Speaking volumes to the tension of the period, Marta Letelier, one of the Letelier family descendants, recorded in her journal, "*Se había suprimido el saludo*" (The [age-old custom of] greeting one another was suppressed).[20] The traditional, submissive salutary bow of the *inquilinos* had given way. Paine peasants defiantly sought to establish new rights. Under Juan Manuel Ortiz's leadership, the Rangue cooperative became part of the forefront of the popular power struggle, assisted by the radical wing of the Popular Unity government, as well as by the extra-parliamentary revolutionary MIR.

News of the September 11, 1973, military coup that began early in the morning in Santiago did not reach Paine until mid-afternoon. That day at dawn, unaware of what was coming to the capital, Gabi's great uncles Rolando and Luis Ortiz and others from Rangue drove their tractors and trucks to the neighboring Mansel hacienda to join approximately 800 peasants and their families in a *toma*.[21] The Mansel hacienda owner had refused to cooperate with the reform legislation, which required that any fallow land beyond an owner's eighty hectares be expropriated and converted into parcels and cooperatives. When the news of the coup arrived, the peasant workers abandoned the *toma* and returned to their homes.

In the month following the coup, the four Ortiz brothers and their fellow workers continued to go each day to the cooperatives, desperately hoping that the expropriations would hold even though other Paine organizers were already being arrested: Over the course of the first week alone, thirteen of those who are now disappeared and murdered were rounded up, including three high school MIR militants who were the first from the town to be executed. In the second week, there would be five more detained–disappeared.

October 1973 proved Paine's most brutal month: between October 2 and October 8, seventeen men were abducted, never to return; from October 13 to October 24, thirty-five, including the Ortiz brothers, were detained, disappeared, and killed. The Paine disappeared and murdered were students, agricultural workers, a handful of small businessmen, and a schoolteacher. Many were political party activists, but several who were not political militants were also murdered. Between mid-September and late October, more than 200 Paine citizens were detained and imprisoned for different lengths of time, from several days, to more than a year.[22] On October 13, the day Juan Manuel and Luis Ortiz were arrested, they were still working at the Rangue cooperative. In late October, two more Ortiz brothers, Rolando and Mauricio Ortiz were also arrested. Mauricio was imprisoned for several months, Rolando for a year-and-a-half.

Following the elimination of the peasant organizers, the dictatorship opted not to return all the expropriated land to the previous owners. In fact, Pinochet decreed that certain expropriations would stand, granting land titles to some tenant farmers and their families, and naming "reserves" that were either returned to the previous owners or granted to administrators of the pre-reform period.

When the landowners and the administrators published the official partitioning of the land, they excluded virtually all families of the imprisoned, executed, and disappeared. According to Decree Law 208 of December 19, 1973, anyone who participated in the *tomas* or who was in any way politically connected to the cooperatives was disqualified from the land rights of the cooperatives. At the Rangue cooperative, approximately twenty-two families gained titles, and most of the titleholders were granted either to former administrators, those disconnected from the peasant struggles, or *afuerinos*, those who came from outside the community.[23]

Grief without mourning

As I research the history of Paine, I am struck by how everything happened so fast. What had been decades, even centuries of much of the same in terms of land tenure and social relations subsequently became a few short years of volatility and drama. Yet a great deal took place in a very brief time span, between 1970 and 1974, and I imagine that for the peasant organizers and militants of Paine, days felt like weeks, weeks like months, and months like years. Long hours were spent designing the plans for the cooperatives, pressing for agreement, electing a leadership, delegating new tasks, securing legal and technical government backing, confronting the establishment, overcoming ongoing obstacles and setbacks. All this and much more required tremendous struggle. Then came the shock of the overwhelming force, rapidity, and brutality of the military reaction, and in two months, many people's lives were eliminated.

Moreover, the traumatic events of Paine happened in a fairly distant past. Yet memories of traumatic moments from many years ago might feel as if they occurred only yesterday. Such memories include when, in the middle of the night, a group of police officers knocked loudly on the door and a loved one was subsequently taken away, or a husband's bullet-riddled body was lying on a forensic table. The intensity of trauma time can both age us and draw us right back to that horrendous instance.

When Gabi's grandfather Luis was taken away, her grandmother, Hilda Inés Cerda, was left with their seven children, including Gabi's father, the oldest, who was fourteen. The youngest child was three-months-old. To survive, the children had to be separated, and two of the girls and one of the boys were sent to relatives in Santiago. Gabi's father and the three youngest remained with Hilda. Soon thereafter, facing utter destitution, Hilda had to sell the tiny land parcel they were awarded. Hilda went to work for a landowning family allied with the forces who had murdered her husband.

Gabi described the many hardships for her grandmother, her father, and the Ortiz family.

> At the time of the coup, the revenge against my grandfather and great-uncle—they were rumored to be the people who were armed—was no joke. And in my rural school as a child, in one class of twenty students, there were six Ortiz cousins, we were all known as the rebellious ones, the smart ones, the black sheep. We are, after all, the grandchildren of the Ortizes.

When I asked her about her relationship with her father today, Gabi looked away. She said that they do not get along so well, they fight a lot, and that there is a lot of bitterness in his life. Gabi said her grandmother told her that when she sold the land, her father wept, as he very much wanted to be the farmer that his father had envisioned for him.

For several of the families of the twenty-two men rounded up on October 16, 1973, three days after the arrests of Juan Manuel and Luis Ortiz, the search to confirm their loved ones' whereabouts continues. This included up until October 2010 the search for Juan Rene's grandfather, René Maureira.[24] Such families do know a great deal about what happened that night, including who participated in the abductions. René Maureira was forty-one years old when Lieutenant Andrés Magaña and his fellow officers dragged him from his home in the middle of that night, in front of his wife and two sons. This was Maureira's second arrest. On the night of September 12, René was detained and held in the National Stadium for almost a month. Sonia Carreño remembers that when her husband was arrested the first time, he assured her that all would be well. She remembers thinking how much she had always respected the military and police as protectors of all law-abiding Chileans. Yet Sonia recounts that René returned home from the Stadium a broken man, only too aware of the brutality of the reaction against them.

In 2005, the judge in charge of the Paine cases secured lieutenant Magaña's confession as the man who directed the October 16 operation. The judge also obtained confessions from several military conscripts who participated that night. Magaña testified that a civilian accompanied him, identifying each house of the persons on the list Magaña carried. The twenty-two men were taken several miles from Paine to a ravine by Lake Rapel. The men were ordered to dig a mass grave. They were then shot and dumped in the grave. In his confession, Magaña claimed that Colonel Leonel Konig instructed him to execute the twenty-two men on site, but that Magaña preferred not to do so in front of the women and children. Instead, Magaña suggested that he kill them elsewhere, and the colonel agreed. In 1979, facing allegations of derogation of duty, Colonel Konig killed himself.[25]

When René Maureira was arrested that second, final time, Sonia began the "ceaseless struggle" of trying to get recognition for her husband's disappearance.[26] The women, who were the companions, wives, sisters, in-laws, and mothers of those who were abducted in Paine, faced a community in fear and a regime that treated them as the enemy. Moreover, as wives and mothers, they largely disavowed their own suffering in order to continue the search and care for their families. Military and police denied their loved ones were in custody, sometimes they laughed in their faces, and at least once, during a meeting among the relatives of the detained–disappeared, police arrested Sonia and three other women. Sonia recalled her refusal to remain in detention quietly, and she began screaming for hours until they released her. Nevertheless, neighbors and townspeople of Paine often thought as Sonia once did, that anyone who was arrested must have done something wrong.

Chilean accounts of the repression are replete with the fact that when individuals were summoned, often through radio announcements or in the newspaper, many simply turned themselves in to the authorities. Parents instructed children to report to the local police precinct to "clear things up." So many Chileans possessed a basic trust in both their own or their family members' innocence and in the rule of law. Over the many years, parents have lived and died with the knowledge that they sent their children to the police and that their children never came back. There are cases in Paine when police came knocking at the house, parents told them where to find their children, or wives told them where to find their husbands. Police then denied a hand in the disappearances, while the families of the missing could find no authority willing to help. On the contrary, parents, wives were ridiculed, threatened, and on their own with grief, loss, and disbelief.

In December 1973, families discovered the dead bodies of fourteen men, Paine agricultural workers and a schoolteacher, who were abducted on and around October 3. The men were dumped in a deep ravine near the Cuesta de Chada, not far from their homes, and the men's relatives followed a rumor that bodies had been found there. Amidst a harrowing encounter with the remains, the Paine families decided not to move the bodies.[27] The families worried that a public exhumation would put many at great risk.

I try to imagine what it must have been like to decide to leave the bodies in the Cuesta de Chada. In addition to the obvious terror in which many people in Paine lived, the decision recalls Dori Laub's notion of a witness-less history. Laub argues that "it was the very circumstance of *being inside the event* that made unthinkable the very notion that a witness could exist . . . The historical imperative to bear witness could essentially *not be met during the actual occurrence*."[28] Paine families lived in close quarters, among loved ones who felt helpless and afraid, among informants both known and unknown, and among the perpetrators, many of whom were known. All were implicated, and many were suspect. The violence of Paine in 1973 was historically unprecedented—the round-ups, families accosted in their homes, men young and old beaten to the ground and yanked into vehicles never to be seen again. It would take years for the women of Paine to make their voices heard in the streets.

In March 1974, three months after the Paine families found and left the bodies of their loved ones in the Cuesta de Chada, a police officer reported that he had come across the same remains, and a judge ordered that the remains be collected and sent to the Medical Legal Service. The relatives went to the forensic agency to reclaim their loved ones, but the agency denied their requests. The families sought the legal counsel of Andrés Aylwin, a congressman before the 1973 military coup who became a human rights lawyer and returned to the congress in 1990. Aylwin began an interminable series of processes of seeking legal remedies—death certificates, in the first instance, and prosecutions of those responsible, which continues to this day.[29] In those first years, only a few of the families were able to secure death certificates. Most families, who knew their loved ones' bodies were in the hands of the Medical Legal Service, waited fourteen years for the certificates.[30]

What effect did this long wait have on the wives and mothers of the men who were killed? What was their grief like? I am particularly haunted by C.S. Lewis's journal of the loss of his wife, "H," to cancer. At the time of H's death, Lewis was a renowned author and a wealthy man, possessed of "resources," which from the outset of his journal, Lewis both recognizes and dismisses, as they do him no good in "getting over" his loss.[31] For Lewis, much of his anguish following H's death leads him to question his faith in God. I am haunted because in spite of Lewis's resources and a supportive environment and society for him, and in spite of the fact that he knew H was dying, the first words of Lewis's journal decry the pure fear of grief:

> No one ever told me that grief felt so much like fear. I am not afraid, but the sensation is like being afraid. The same fluttering in the stomach, the same restlessness, the yawning. I keep on swallowing.[32]

For Lewis, grief as fear is the total uncertainty of how to proceed, how to live one's daily life in the absence of one's life's partner. Imagine what the grief experienced by the families of Paine must have felt in the context of real threat, a hostile environment, and the shock of having loved ones suddenly taken away.

Students of grief once believed that the aggrieved pass through stages, that there is an identifiable pattern, termed, "the seven stages of grief." While today few grief scholars wish to be associated with a "stage-ist" approach to grief, most recognize that there are discernible emotions that most grievers experience. These include shock, denial, pain, guilt, anger, depression, and loneliness. Moreover, according to the conventional wisdom, at some point the aggrieved are expected to experience "the upward turn"—they will work through grief, they will accept, and ultimately, they will hope again.[33] Even the most upbeat popular literature does not claim that grievers experience some kind of return to a pre-tragedy life, or that happiness is just around the bend. Yet there is an underlying assumption that grief must be overcome in order for life to continue.

As I think about the grieving of Paine, I am torn about this. What is clear is that the Chilean state and society must recognize, must acknowledge the families' grievous realities.

US writer Joan Didion and her husband and fellow writer John Dunne faced a medical crisis with their daughter, Quintana, a woman in her early twenties. Five days into the crisis, while Quintana lay unconscious at the hospital, Dunne suffered a fatal heart attack. In her moving and often jarring account, *The Year of Magical Thinking*, Didion writes that she did not allow herself to mourn the loss of her husband while her daughter lay hospitalized. Didion distinguishes between grief, that panoply of raw emotions that followed her husband's death, from mourning, which Didion sees as the more conscious act of grieving.

Didion's mourning of her husband, it seems to me, begins several months after his death, when Didion is fairly confident that her daughter is on a clear path to rehabilitation. Didion seems to allow herself to mourn mainly through reading—reading what others had written about Dunne, Dunne's own writings, and a vast range of literature, from poetry to medical journals, about death and medical procedures. All of Didion's reading seems to be a searching for a way to connect with him, to trace and pinpoint when Dunne might have known he was dying, and to understand what he might have been feeling those last weeks, days, and moments of his life. All of this appears aimed at somehow bringing him back to her.

For Didion in those months before she allowed herself to mourn, grief involved her consciously trying to banish him (and her daughter) from her mind and her memories, avoiding particular routes and habits, for example. Obviously this proved impossible, as she had lived virtually day in and day out with him, for forty years. She simply could not control her memories, and they shared a very full life together. Mourning, on the other hand, recognized that Didion needed to dwell in her memories of Dunne, both because she recognized there was no way around this, and because she appreciated, consciously or not, that through mourning she would be trying to bring her husband into her world in a way that was less "irrational," "fragile," or "raw."[34] It seems that for Didion, grief is feeling the "unending absence," "the void," "the permanent impassibility of the divide," while mourning is entering into a space and time that allowed her to process and accept the reality of these profound feelings.[35]

It finally hits me, quite painfully, that the Paine widows, mothers, were simply unable, not allowed, did not allow themselves, to mourn. All of the symptoms of grief—shock, pain, anger, depression—were unending, even exacerbated over years by false leads, official unresponsiveness and hostility, and societal denial and numbness. How can there be "uplift" in such conditions? How can one deny the reality of the pain they suffered? And the children, those who were young, teenagers, or young men and women, grew up amidst perpetual familial traumatic grief. The children matured fast, they had to help care for the family. For this generation, anger and depression prevail, expressed privately, behind closed doors.

Accounts of grief and mourning indicate that an integral part of the mourning process is the space and capacity to give testimony. Joan Didion processes through reading and writing. She finds her voice, her subject-position, and she writes a book that communicates her testimony to an enormous audience. We can see that Didion has found a space for enunciation. For the women of Paine, the memorial would become one way to give testimony, to take a major creative hand in commemorating their loss.

Paine families began building the space with one another as they journeyed on the frustrating search for answers.[36] Several Paine families, such as the Ortiz families, the Lazo families, and the Muñoz families, were already related by kinship. Four brothers—Jorge Hernán (age 28), Mario Enrique (age 30), Ramiro Antonio (age 32), and Silvestre René Muñoz Peñaloza (age 33)—were abducted, never to return. Their wives often traveled together to the detention centers and the morgue, trying to spare Mercedes Muñoz Peñaloza, the men's mother, the horrors of the search.[37] In addition to her four sons, Muñoz lost a son-in-law and the husband of her oldest granddaughter—six men in all, all agricultural workers. A few Paine families participated and gained strength from meetings and actions in Santiago.

It would be 1989, sixteen years after the abductions, that Paine women first publicly demonstrated for truth and justice for the victims of Paine, *in* Paine itself.[38] On the day of that first march, the women recount that at first there were no more than six of them in the street, and they were under pressure by the police to move to the sidewalk. The women bravely refused, and gradually the march grew larger, numbering close to sixty or seventy men, women, and children.[39]

In 1990, shortly after Paine's first public march and the new government assumed political leadership, Chilean interior secretary Belisario Velasco announced that the government forensic office found three plastic bags filled with the bones and detritus corresponding to approximately fourteen people, and that the bag had been sent by police from the Paine precinct. Velasco stated that at least four of the skeletal remains showed evidence of gunshot wounds. Newly appointed special minister for human rights violations cases, judge Germán Hermosilla, began an immediate investigation, ordering the initiation of several exhumation projects throughout the country, including a return to excavate in Paine. Because of the nature of the Cuesta de Chada burial and exhumation, the new government was able to confirm comparatively quickly what the Paine families knew many years ago. Fourteen men from Paine had been executed and dumped in the Cuesta de Chada.[40]

The 1989 public demonstration and the new government's 1990 confirmation of the Paine remains gave new impetus for action. Relatives marched again in 1990, this time to demand justice in relation to the exhumations. In 1991, Chile's official Truth and Reconciliation Report named Paine as the site with the most detained–disappeared and executed of any region per capita in the country. As Juan René Maureira argues, however, the public revelations and the exhumations also had a chilling, even terrifying effect on many Paine families. It drove home the horror of the loved ones' deaths. It was like reliving the experiences with a new certainty and dread.

Maureira's grandmother Sonia said that seeing with her own eyes the bones from the morgue and the remains from the Cuesta de Chada, including remains of men who had been with her husband on the same night he was abducted, forced her to admit to herself for the first time, truly, that the Chilean authorities were actually capable of having brutally murdered René and many others.[41] Until that moment, on some level, Sonia had resisted such an admission. She now granted room for the strong possibility that René was murdered, that she needed to search for his remains, and that the perpetrators of these horrendous crimes, some of whom she knew, had to be held accountable.

In the post-dictatorial period, and as they became adults, the children of Paine's missing and executed joined their mothers' long struggle for truth and justice. Soon the grandchildren would also search, and more deeply. They were questioning the silences and the fragmented accounts at home as well as out in the world. These descendants brought fresh perspectives and ideas, and they wanted to move beyond the painful past.

Postmemory and the transmission of grief

In the literature on the transmission of traumatic memories across generations, there is tension among understandings of what is received, what is conveyed, what is silent, and what is obsessively present. The challenge, it seems to me, is to move from a focus on the generation of those who were killed, to a focus on what it is that the descendants feel, seek, or demand, as well as what the implications are for a commemorative politics. Both Marianne Hirsch's reflections on the Holocaust and postmemory and Alejandra Oberti's work on memory transmission in post-dictatorial Argentina are insightful contributions to such understandings.

Hirsch writes that children of Holocaust victims "inherit a horrific, unknown, and unknowable past that their parents were not meant to survive."[42] Such children, who later become artists, writers, and scholars, produce works that reflect their intense search for meaning in the wake of so much pain and loss:

> They are shaped by the child's confusion and responsibility, by the desire to repair, and by the consciousness that the child's own existence may well be a form of compensation for unspeakable loss. Loss of family, of home, of a feeling of belonging and safety in the world 'bleed' from one generation to the next . . .[43]

In the absence of living relatives and amidst such loss and the pain of those who did survive, Holocaust descendants must often rely on broader, even popularized stories and renderings that communicate the horror of the genocide. The renderings include well-known photographs from the ghettos and concentration camps, which the younger generations then transpose, as screens for projecting, for imagining, for making sense of their own family histories and identities. Like the second generation of Chileans, Holocaust survivors who are very young children are denied their childhood. The "bleeding" across generations captures why it might often fall to the third generation to struggle to recuperate memories beyond the painful wound of absence.

As an important comparative case to be explored in greater depth in my next chapter, Argentina brings into sharp relief conceptually and artistically the meanings of brutal repression, familial grief, and the enduring search for ways to mourn for the descendants of the disappeared and murdered during Argentina's 1976–83 military dictatorship. For our purposes, there are several distinctions worth noting. While my focus in this chapter is on the repression that took place in a rural community against older as well as young peasant organizers, for Argentina much of the attention around a commemorative politics focuses on the youthfulness of those who were disappeared. This is best symbolized by Argentina's Mothers of the Plaza of Mayo, who are perhaps the most well-known association of relatives of the disappeared in the world, and by the young faces on the placards that the mothers hold high.

Moreover, in contrast to Paine, both the analytical literature and the artistic commemorative renderings of Argentina tend to emanate from the cosmopolitan capital of Buenos Aires, as well as from Argentina's middle class. (This also holds true for Chile, where most discussions of memory and commemoration focus on Santiago, Chile's capital.) Finally, in contrast to Paine, many of the Argentine disappeared are women. The artistic and analytical shifts of age, place, class, and gender between my study of Paine and those I draw from Argentina are thus important to note. The distinctions also make the Paine women and the *Paine Memorial* all the more remarkable. Nevertheless, the two countries share fundamentally similar political trajectories of democracy, dictatorship, repression, and transition, with comparable experiences of cross-generational struggle, loss, mourning, and activism.

In her study of the inter-generational transmission of traumatic memories in Argentine politically militant families, Alejandra Oberti emphasizes the "active" rather than "inherited" transmission of memories, even when there is a great deal of family silence.[44] More often than not, the transmissions come in bits and pieces, sometimes contradicting one another. Psychoanalyst Jacque Hassoun's conceptualization of memories moving discursively within families across generations like "contraband," serves Oberti's study well, as she wishes to understand what is transmitted when violence disrupts the flow.[45] Contraband memory transmission connotes clandestine activity, furtiveness, and risk. Oberti's interviews and analysis of Argentine children of the disappeared help us understand how and why new generations, in Argentina, Chile, and elsewhere, demand to know more about the lives of their parents who were killed, as well as why they are not satisfied with passive presentations of their loved ones as victims rather than subjects.

Often the only direct physical connection for children of the disappeared to their parents is a family photograph, taken at a moment when the children are too young to remember the photo's context. This creates a "frozen" sense of their parents; the children see themselves next to a father or mother (or both) who has disappeared, and they are haunted by not remembering the circumstances surrounding the photograph. The children want to "fill in the blanks."[46]

Hirsch, too, shows how family photographs that include those lost to the Holocaust work both to connect and to distance subsequent generations. Those in the photographs are both immediate and elusive, "ghostly revenants from an irretrievably lost past world."[47] In his photographic series *Ausencias*, Argentine artist Gustavo Germano, whose brother was a political militant and is now a *desaparecido*, literally creates the absence of the disappeared loved one in the present.[48] Germano selects original photographs that are informal, ordinary, light, happy snapshots of siblings, sons and daughters, mothers and fathers, that include the missing loved ones. He then re-photographs the scene, placing the surviving family members in roughly the same positions where they once sat, or stood, or lay, this time without the disappeared family member or members. Germano's juxtaposition of original family photographs with his contemporary re-creations is an unbelievably jarring commemoration of absence.[49] His commemorative work sheds brilliant light on the issues that Paine families faced as they imagined and struggled over how to counter absence with presence.

Family photographs can be important points of departure in children's search for more information, for explanations. Oberti finds that the children of disappeared Argentine militants struggle to discover as much as they can about their parents, in good part to establish an "anchor" of their own origins. This desire to learn more also helps them separate, or become autonomous selves within the family, and it differentiates the children of the disappeared from others in the family who have been comparatively silent about the disappeared parents.

In Paine one sees the constancy of the search. Their search for meaning is lifelong, continues from generation to generation, and is not always successful. Several women who were mothers of the disappeared men of Paine died before the remains of their loved ones were unearthed. Searching implies movement, progression, even if a search may prove fitful, halting, and uncertain. Searching is about following paths, and about integrating experiences, ideas, and emotions into our cognitive selves.

Yet sometimes, as was often the case for the women of Paine, it is very difficult to detect any progression whatsoever. In Chilean filmmaker Patricio Guzmán's 2010 documentary, *Nostalgia por la luz*, we encounter seventy-year-old Violeta Berríos, who has been searching, literally, for loved ones in northern Chile's Atacama desert for some twenty years.[50] Berríos does not accept the military's assertion that "they were thrown into the sea." She feels it is quite possible that in fact loved ones were buried in the desert, a soil so dry that it has an eerie way of conserving the corpses. In 1991, the remains of several missing Chilean activists were discovered in the northern desert region of Pisagua, and Berríos has every reason to believe more are missing in the desert.

"Sometimes I feel like an idiot," Berríos says, "because I keep asking questions, questions, questions, and in the end, no one gives me the answers I want." Berríos's explanation of her search is both calm and disturbing. On the one hand, Berríos says, "[the authorities] taught me not to believe [them]," but on the other, she doggedly pursues claims also given by the authorities. Berríos says that if she is told, "They were thrown onto the top of the mountain," she will find a way to search the top of the mountain. "It will be difficult," Berríos acknowledges, "but hope gives you a lot of strength," to continue the search.[51]

A post-nostalgic commemorative politics

Like the title of Guzmán's documentary, *Nostalgia por la luz*, there is something about Chilean commemorative processes that seems to elicit an overwhelming nostalgia. It is clear that commemoration in general is often nostalgic. Yet retrieving the Chilean past in relation to the present consistently evokes a claim that those who struggle for memory in Chile are too frozen in a bygone era. And indeed, I have often been struck by the notable wistfulness in the way many Chileans discuss the past, not simply in the stereotypical sense we associate with older people. Eliana Loveluck, a Chilean, a daughter of exiles, who has lived in the United States since her teenage years in the early 1970s, helped me think about this. Eliana agreed that Chileans are both accused of and in fact appear to be more nostalgic about the distant past than Chile's South American neighbors, who have similarly experienced the breakdown of democratic regimes, the brutality of military dictatorships, and processes of re-democratization and coming to terms with painful pasts. She argues that Chileans' pronounced nostalgia has to do with the fact that the collective historical dream of moving toward a more egalitarian society was so brutally smashed, and the contrast between Chile's pre-dictatorial past and Chile's present is so stark.[52]

This is Paine's trajectory. The once predominantly rural area experienced a brief, dramatic redistribution of power. The military dictatorship abruptly reversed its course. Over the past thirty years, land speculation, the commercialization of agriculture, and some modest local tourist development characterize the region, and the town of Paine has become a bedroom community for the expanding metropolis of Santiago. Paine's physical terrain is virtually unrecognizable from that of Paine of the 1960s and 1970s. And the peasant struggles have been erased.

Nevertheless, many of the family members remain. Juan René Maureira's grandmother Sonia still operates the grocery store. One of her two sons, Juan René's uncle Juan Leonardo, has become a local community leader, crucial to organizing the *Memorial of Paine*. And what began as a small, underground gathering of families of the disappeared and murdered of Paine became the strong Association of Families of the Detained–Disappeared and Executed of Paine (AFDD-Paine). The organization meets formally once a month, and an average of thirty to forty members, spanning three generations, consistently attends and participates. In addition to their ongoing demands for investigations and accountability, the AFDD-Paine has successfully labored to elaborate a lasting commemoration.

In the year 2000, as part of a halting but continuing effort to overcome their fear through collective cultural initiatives, AFDD-Paine members conducted a survey of the Paine community to determine the number of descendants directly related to the seventy men who were detained–disappeared and executed. The decision to carry out the survey was also indicative of the children and grandchildren's increasing influence in the direction of the AFDD-Paine. While the AFDD-Paine's traditional objectives remain "Justice, Truth, and Memory," the organization added: "Construction of a Memorial for the community of Paine, Integration of the Third Generation, Integration with the community, Make what happened in Paine known in Chile and abroad."[53]

The 2000 survey determined that from the first generation to the third generation, there were more than a thousand direct descendants of those who were disappeared and killed. The descendants would come to be symbolized in the *Paine Memorial* by 1,000 pine logs, minus seventy logs that recognized the dead and disappeared. In place of the missing seventy logs, the family members created colorful mosaics, filled with iconography, to represent a living memory of each loved one. The pines were cut to conceptualize the Andes horizon, an eternal feature of Chile's landscape.

The *Paine Memorial* represents the accomplishments of three generations' long struggle to memorialize their loved ones. The 1,000 logs and the seventy mosaics represent Paine's direct descendants of the disappeared and killed, enjoined with those they lost. The contrast between Spain's statist, dark, and imposing *Valley of the Fallen* and the grassroots-inspired *Paine Memorial* could not be starker. And while the descendants and loved ones of Peru's dead and disappeared have come to identify with Lika Mutal's *The Eye that Cries*, the inter-generational working through is far less central to the Mutal sculpture. Moreover, the tensions among opposing political forces in state and society that visibly swirl around *The Eye that Cries* memorial are not apparent in the *Paine Memorial*.

But it was still a difficult path to negotiate the memorial the Paine families wanted. Members of the second generation were most responsible for securing state financing and support for the memorial. The fact that Paine was the official site of the highest number of disappeared per capita in Chile made the memorial request a clear choice for government sponsorship.

Figure 4.1 Paine Memorial Forest (photo by Katherine Hite).

The confluence of generational turnover in the leadership of the Association of the Families of the Disappeared of Paine, coupled with a fairly recent official appreciation of the potential political value of commemoration, ensured the memorial's coming to fruition. The AFDD-Paine first approached the Human Rights Program of the Ministry of the Interior. Once the Program approved the idea, the AFDD-Paine began to work with the Ministry of Public Works to elaborate the design and implement construction.

Nevertheless, moving from agreement to implementation and maintenance has been and continues to be a long road through bureaucratic hurdles, many agencies, and other obstacles. For example, although the government recognized the need for "psychological accompaniment" of family members, the initial route for addressing this was unsuccessful. The government sent to Paine a group of young psychology students to lead group therapy sessions. To family members, the therapy sessions felt like a waste of time. One Paine participant recounted how families ended up having to console the crying psychologists. Ultimately, they sent the psychology students away, and then continued the important work with the artists, whose input they realized that they valued more.

In the course of negotiating the plans and funding for the memorial, Chilean President Ricardo Lagos (2000–06) invited the representatives of the AFDD-Paine to La Moneda presidential palace, where the president gave them a personal tour. In the wake of the 1998 arrest of former dictator Augusto Pinochet and with the dawn of a new millennium, the Chilean state began, with Lagos, to claim a politics of commemoration. Lagos and his advisers recognized that icons, such as former president Salvador Allende, could be re-appropriated, toward a memory of democratic, even heroic loss. After more than a decade of uncomfortable silence regarding the relationship with this socialist leader and president, Lagos reclaimed Allende as a statesman. On September 11, 2003, the thirtieth anniversary of the coup, Lagos embraced the statue of Allende that stood outside the presidential palace, and he reopened the door of Morandé 80, a door that had been sealed shut by the dictatorship in the wake of Allende's last stance there.[54] On March 9, 2006, his last day in office, Lagos landed by helicopter in Paine's local stadium and traveled to the memorial site to witness and publicize the memorial work in progress.[55]

The Association of Families of the Detained–Disappeared continues to struggle to secure the basic fiscal support necessary to maintain the site.[56] Rather than implement the group's original design for an ample meeting place and cultural center, government officials installed a shipping container—a trailer-like rectangular structure that conveyed a temporary and precarious feel. The AFDD-Paine has made the container work, and the monthly organization meetings once held in a cramped room next to Sonia Carreño's store now take place on the memorial site.

To revitalize and, in an important sense, to more deeply politicize the Paine commemorative process, a group of Paine's grandchildren of the detained–disappeared and executed, including Juan René and Gabi, depicted in Figures 4.2 and 4.3, organized *La Tercera Generación*, The Third Generation. The Third Generation emphasizes beauty and joy, continuity with the past while fully celebrating the present. Juan René recognizes the tension that flares from time to time between the grandchildren and grandparents about how to remember their loved ones. For the grandparents, memories of their loved ones tend to emphasize their deaths and disappearances, the grief associated with the loss, while The Third Generation urges recuperating memories of their loved ones' lived experiences in order to know them, as human beings.

The Third Generation formed the Youth Orchestra of Paine, composed primarily of grandchildren of the disappeared or executed. During the mosaic making for the Memorial each Saturday, the Third Generation ensured there was music. Third Generation members have visited elementary, high school, and university classrooms to share Paine's history and work. Together with the Association of Detained–Disappeared of Paine, the Third Generation has hosted dozens of Chilean and international group visits to the memorial, including, in March 2008, a visit I organized of forty-three students and faculty from Vassar College. It was the *Paine Memorial*'s first public act for a group of outsiders, a beautiful, moving ceremony of song and testimony, accompanied by the photographs of the victims. After the ceremony, four generations

Figure 4.2 Juan René Maureira (photo by Katherine Hite).

Figure 4.3 Gabriela Ortiz (photo by Katherine Hite).

of Paine families, including a few very young great-grandchildren, gathered around the mosaics of their loved ones to explain the icons and symbols to small groups of Vassar members.

In light of this long inter-generational struggle, the pastiche of the different images in the mosaics becomes so powerful. For example, the mosaic that the Maureira family made that commemorates René Maureira includes a representation of the grocery store Maureira founded, *Mapa*. There is a truck that represents the first truck Maureira bought with his own money. The truck also symbolizes Maureira's role as a coordinator of the JAP, the Popular Unity government-established agency that distributed basic goods amidst private sector and middle-class hoarding. In one corner of the Maureira mosaic is a house with the name Torca, which represents the first house René and Sonia shared as newlyweds. Torca is the name of a small town in the south, and René and Sonia left Torca to settle in Paine.

Grandsons Juan René and Emerson explained that during the course of making the Maureira mosaic, children and grandchildren often heard, for the first time, the stories, even the favorite jokes, of the loved ones they didn't know. Sonia remembered that once as she and her husband were reminiscing about their first little home together in Torca, she said to him, "And that's where I first served you tea, where I came to know you." And as she recounted this to the family working on the mosaic, her son, Juan René's uncle, said,

Figure 4.4 Detail of the mosaic commemorating Roberto Serrano Galaz (photo by Gabriela Ortiz).

Figure 4.5 Detail of the mosaic commemorating Laureano Quiroz Pezoa,
            recognizing his leadership in the Popular Unity government's basic
            staples distribution program, the JAP (photo by Gabriela Ortiz).

"Ah, so this is where you conceived me," And the grandmother said, "Yes, this is where you came into being."

Gabriela recounted a different story in the course of the mosaic-making: One of her uncles said to her grandmother, apparently only half in jest, "Mom, where do we put a bottle symbolizing the times Dad came home drunk after a night in the bar?" Not all memories made the cut. The mosaics communicate work—tractors, a hoe, favorite past-times—a soccer ball, a guitar, and political activism. One of the mosaics commemorates a high school student in the MIR through images of the MIR leadership. The students were the first to fall, executed right on the street. Some of the mosaics have doves, others a night sky, or a crying woman, hands outreached, tears of blood.

For Juan René, the exciting, meaningful work of his generation is taking place in the arena of popular education, where university students organize workshops and courses in working-class neighborhoods to construct collective histories of the community.[57] Juan René described one such effort, El Cordón Popular de Educación, a name that borrows from the worker-run *cordones industriales*, the "industrial belts" of the Popular Unity period.

Popular education and participatory community histories clearly inspire the *Tercera Generación's* efforts and hopes for the *Paine Memorial*. In contrast to Villa Grimaldi, a Chilean former concentration camp that has become a National Historic Site and a human rights center, the *Paine Memorial* focuses on the people of Paine, where students can come to do their homework, and

Figure 4.6 Detail of the mosaic of Luis Gaete (photo by Katherine Hite).

Figure 4.7 Mrs. Luz Castro working on the mosaic with her grandson (photo by Alex Chelew).

Figure 4.8 Mrs. Silvia Vargas and members of her family preparing tiles for the
mosaic (photo by Alex Chelew).

where cultural activities of the town can take place. Gabi Ortíz has been trying
to spearhead a library as part of the *Paine Memorial*'s *Centro de Acción Social*.
Through recording and sharing the history of Paine, she and The Third
Generation seek to re-politicize the community. "There is still so much fear
in this community," Gabi said. "You know, my uncle, whose father was
murdered, has been to our memorial only once, and he always says to me to
stay out of politics. I just smile at him."[58]

More recently, members of *La Tercera Generación*, including Gabriela and
her cousins, have inserted in the mosaics small plaques with the names and a
brief message from the grandchildren themselves. The mosaics of Paine not
only remember individuals. In a strong sense, the mosaics construct the
individuals as well, particularly as one thinks about what it means for
grandchildren to participate in the remembering of men they never knew.[59]
The *Paine Memorial* materializes, it presences, what had been absence—the
grief, loss, years of struggle.[60]

The official commemorative ceremony took place several months after the
Vassar visit. Chilean President Michelle Bachelet presided. While relations
between the Paine group and the state have proved volatile, Juan René captures
the importance of the state's strong validation of the memorial:

Those most affected in our community, those families most hurt, most afraid, feel the support of the state. Now they are believed. It's solid. And those not directly affected, or those who said, "they must have been guilty of something, it must have been for a good reason," now recognize how horrendous it really was. Official visits help with this. The state is making amends, re-dignifying our loved ones.[61]

5   The globality of art and memory making

The *bicis* of Fernando Traverso

Perhaps I had been reading too much about monuments. The first thing that occurred to me as I viewed Fernando Traverso's stenciled bicycle silhouettes in a show in New York City was how the bicycles' uniformity was a provocative twist on the uniformity of the anonymous US civil war soldier statues.[1] The anonymous soldiers are erected in towns across America to remember local heroes, but the statues also serve to mark US territories as one, united nation. Most of the soldier statues were mass-produced, and it is difficult to distinguish between a confederate and a union soldier, though the two are not the same. In the early twentieth century, US northern and southern towns placed them in central squares rather than in cemeteries, to project patriotic sacrifice by the Everyman.[2] Similarly, in a patriotic reference to his nation of Argentina, Traverso's "In Memory" installation art piece used the Argentine flag's particular sky blue for the flags that serve as backdrops for various black silk-screened bicycles. The *bicis*, the bikes, remember several people he knew, and Traverso proclaims their national sacrifice. I would later learn that for Traverso, Argentines' right to wave their political flags in public, a right denied them during the dictatorships of Juan Onganía (1966–73) and the military juntas of El Proceso (1976–83), was something the artist considered fundamental, something sacred.[3]

Traverso explains the concept behind his *bicis*: During the last Argentine dictatorship in the late 1970s, more than 350 citizens of his home city of Rosario, Argentina, disappeared. Many who disappeared were activists in the resistance movement, and they often used bicycles to get around. During the course of the dictatorship, increasing numbers of bicycles were left abandoned in a driveway, outside a home, along a curb. Their riders, including several of Traverso's comrades, were never seen again. Traverso's first *bici* project in Rosario was to stencil, number, and photograph the *bicis* throughout the city, until he reached number 350.

Traverso insists his *bicis* are counter-monuments. "I detest monuments, I don't believe in them, I even protest against them," Traverso told me.[4] "Monuments meant to remember people just end up killing them all over again." Traverso described a collective action he helped organize to protest his city's decision to erect in 2008 a monument to Ernesto Ché Guevara on the occasion of Ché's eightieth birthday. Ché was born in Rosario.[5] The monument, a rather improbable likeness of Ché, now stands in a park along Rosario's riverbank, not far from Traverso's home. The day I visited the monument, shortly after its inauguration, two young men asked for assistance to have their pictures taken with the statue. The young men struck serious poses.

Not long ago, the German counter-monument artist Horst Hoheissel visited Rosario, and Traverso spoke at length with him about the commonalities of their work. Hoheissel is best known for his provocative "negative form monument," which replicates a "Jews Fountain" destroyed under the Nazi regime. Hoheissel inverted the replica of the fountain and sunk it underground. Like Traverso's *bicis*, the German artist's projects are often dynamic, interactive, turning the memorial viewers into the memorial participants.[6] "Horst gave me a way to theorize what I was already doing by instinct," Traverso said. "I create counter-monuments."

Traverso and I sat at his kitchen table. His modest house also serves as his studio, and Traverso's paintings, stencils, and renderings occupy every inch of wall space. Up the stairs is Traverso's workroom, and it opens out to a patio roof that allows him to spread his stencils and paints over large canvases. For the past twenty-five years, Traverso has worked full-time in Rosario's provincial hospital of Santa Fe, and for the past several years he has been a technician in the primary care unit. Beyond the fact that his job provides his

Figure 5.1 *Bici* on a garage door (photo by Katherine Jensen).

Figure 5.2 *Bici* on a store wall (photo by Katherine Hite).

chief income, Traverso feels deeply connected to his hospital work and colleagues. He considers himself a worker who also does art. He does not want to depend on art sales to earn a living. Traverso seeks independence from the confines and pretenses of the art world, to work with what he has, "which is very little."

Several times during our visit Traverso apologized to me for not being formally educated, which made me smile as he proceeded to recommend recent memoirs, analyses, and fiction that would help me understand the politics of memory of contemporary Argentina. One was *La casa de los conejos* (*The House of Rabbits*), a best-selling semi-autobiographical novel about a little girl who grew up fast as the daughter of guerrillas in the Argentine underground. Traverso instructed me to read *La casa de los conejos* on my plane ride home, as it "reads quickly and is perfect for the plane." He was right.

La casa de los conejos contributes to current debates about the nature and role of guerrilla action in the years before the 1976 *coup d'état*. The name of the novel comes from the intense, tenuous period in which the girl, her mother, and other comrades lived in a house where they used rabbit hutches as a cover for an enormous hidden printing press. The novel captures the anxieties, the sense of responsibility, and the little girl's struggle to be unusually mature as she confronts her father's imprisonment, her mother's clandestinity, the awful mood swings of those in hiding around her, and the tensions surrounding her daily life. Argentina has experienced an explosion of accounts of the 1960s and 1970s urban guerrilla movement. The country's post-dictatorial politics of memory debates have assumed distinct emphases over time, and here we will examine these debates in ways that both echo post-fascist and post-authoritarian experiences elsewhere and that forge new ground, pioneering global commemorative connection and promise.

Traverso's artistic political sustenance comes in good part from his collaboration with other artists, cultural workers as he sees them, primarily at home in Rosario but also around the world. Beyond Rosario, Traverso has worked with artist–student–activist groups in Chile, Colombia, Mexico, Spain, and the US. His website opens with the artist demonstrating in fast motion how he uses the stencil to create a black silhouette of a *bici* on a white wall. The website provides a link with instructions on how to download the stencil, and all Traverso asks in return is to be sent a photograph with the newly stenciled image, wherever it has been enacted. Traverso's website is filled with photographs of people young and old, on various continents, stenciling the *bicis*, with and without him. The global reach of Traverso's *bicis* is facilitated by the artist's solidaristic spirit, easy access to the *bici* design both conceptually and practically, and a dynamic taking up of the *bicis* by dozens of communities around the world, toward diverse meanings. The *bici* memorials of Traverso both mourn the sacrifice, the failed projects of the past, and establish politically minded global connection, participation, and possibility.

Politics of memory passages in Argentina

Approximately one million people live in Rosario, Argentina's third largest city. Like most of the country, Rosario's is a boom and bust economy. It is located in the province of Santa Fe, a region that depends on agro-industry, cattle, oil refineries, and petrochemical processing plants. Rosario is home to a major university and to rich urban cultural and civic life. Political progressives have generally governed Rosario. The city's robust performing and visual arts frequently depict Argentina's brutal dictatorial past.

In the course of my stay in the city, I asked lots of people about whether they knew the *bicis*, and if so, what the bicycles meant to them. I met no one who was unfamiliar with the *bicis*. For many, many citizens of Rosario, the *bicis* that dot the city evoke solidarity with their riders. Rosarinos speak appreciatively of the *bicis*, as a positive dimension of their urban landscape.

Rubén Chababo is the director of Rosario's Museum of Memory and a leading thinker on conceptualizing artistic spaces of memory in Latin America and elsewhere. The Museum of Memory was Argentina's first officially sponsored national museum to focus on the atrocities of the dictatorship, to offer a sophisticated, nuanced narration of the repressive years. It opened in 2004. For several years the museum was housed in a municipal building while a coalition of municipal, grassroots, and civic leaders fought successfully to create a permanent museum in the building that once housed the Army's Second Corps Division headquarters. Under Chababo's directorial leadership, the permanent Museum of Memory was inaugurated in December 2010, designed on the premise that memory institutions should always seek to provoke questions, to confront and defy the "great ghost of museumification."[7] Chababo resisted the museum's imposing a chronology of the Argentine conflict and repression, which to his mind implied some kind of "before" and "after," raising far too many problems of interpretation. Rather, the Museum is organized aesthetically around several themes, including clandestine imprisonment, kidnapped and illegally adopted children of mothers who are *desaparecidas*,[8] the struggles for truth and justice, and bearing witness.[9]

Chababo took me on a walking tour of Rosario. As we set out on our tour from what was then the temporary museum, Chababo said, with a slightly ironic tone, given our point of departure, that Rosario's memory art is not in the museum, really, but out in the streets.[10] As we walked, Chababo explained his city's abundant graffiti iconography. Among the many iconic symbols were references to workers' struggles, generals on trial, rock musicians, political parties, and the white handkerchiefs of the mothers of the disappeared. We also encountered several *bicis*.

In Argentina's 1984 official truth commission report, *Nunca Más* (*Never Again*), Rosario earns the notorious distinction as the first documented site of a case of a disappearance. Twenty-three-year-old Angel "Tacuarita" Brandazza, a Peronist university student militant known for his work in marginal neighborhoods of the city, was kidnapped and disappeared at the hands of armed government security forces. While this was an exceptional case in 1972, the disappearance came to represent a frequent practice by the end of 1974, when Argentina was still nominally a constitutional government.

The years leading to the 1976 military coup proved politically volatile, polarizing, marked in 1973 by democratic elections after several years of military rule, the return from two decades in exile of longtime leader Juan Perón, his death in mid-1974, and a scramble for power by Peronist allies and foes on the left and the right. In good part a legacy of Perón's 1946–55 presidency and the building of a major popular base, Argentina's organized urban and rural working class was the strongest in Latin America. Memorial struggles in Argentina today are often related to Peronist alliances and divisions and to intense identifications with the working class.

The 1970s was also the period of the visible emergence of an urban guerrilla movement, chiefly the left Peronist-allied Montoneros, but also the People's Revolutionary Army (ERP), prevalent in Rosario. The Montoneros' first claimed guerrilla action, the assassination of former anti-Peronist dictator, General Pedro Aramburu (1955–58), took place in 1970, amidst the second anti-Peronist military regime (1966–73). There was a deliberately dramatic character to the revolutionary politics of the Montoneros. During the 1970s, the Montoneros and the ERP were responsible for kidnappings and assassinations of right-wing military officers, politicians, diplomats, and national and international corporate executives. The guerrillas raided military bases throughout the country and bombed multinational company headquarters, banks, and other symbols of capital.

As in much of the world, the late 1960s and early 1970s were also a period of significant radical artistic movements, intensely intertwined with the politics of that period. The most famous series of Argentine collective artistic actions occurred in 1968, when a group of well-known Rosarino and Buenos Aires avant garde artists exposed and denounced the impoverishment of the rural province of Tucumán and, implicitly, Argentine bourgeois economic and cultural institutions themselves. Tucumán was home to small farmers and sugar factory workers newly subjected to Operation Tucumán, a neoliberal drive of the Juan Onganía dictatorship to privatize and centralize the sugar cane and citrus-growing region for commercial exports. Working chiefly with union and political organizers, the artists used paint, photography, texts, and videos—a multiplicity of visual forms—to document the deterioration of basic living standards for ordinary people in Tucumán, as well as the largesse of the region's wealthy that globalization inevitably produces. The artist collective, known as "Tucumán Arde" (Tucumán is Burning), mounted a series of exhibits in Rosario, Santa Fe, and ultimately, in Buenos Aires, where the exhibit was immediately shut down by the authorities.

An important aspect of the 1960 and 1970s radicalization was the rebellion of many artists against producing art itself, which they determined was a bourgeois enterprise. Such was the case for Juan Pablo Renzi, a well-known Rosarino artist who stopped painting for several years. Renzi's 1968 stickers and sketches deeply influenced Traverso's artistic trajectory.[11] At least two of the Tucumán Arde artists, including renowned Rosarino painter Eduardo Favario, joined the ERP. Favario died in a 1975 shoot-out with security forces in a rural area of Santa Fe.[12]

In June 1973, an estimated three million or more supporters gathered at Argentina's Ezeiza airport to welcome Juan Perón's return from exile. Violence broke out, and several Montoneros were killed. The event became known as the Ezeiza massacre, and it marked the end of any conceivable alliance of left and right Peronists. Meanwhile, Perón himself publicly broke with the Montoneros shortly before he died. Under Perón's widow Isabel, who assumed the presidency in the aftermath of his death, government security forces created the Argentine Anticommunist Alliance, or the Triple A, a paramilitary unit that systematically hunted down and murdered Montonero and ERP guerrillas and their suspected allies. At the time of the military coup, there were already more than 5,000 political prisoners. Government kidnapping and disappearance became systematic, a virtual industry with enormous repressive machinery, and scores of Argentine citizens were its victims. While scattered guerrilla actions continued through the 1970s, from early on the guerrillas proved no match for the Triple A, much less for the military juntas' 1976–83 "National Reorganization Process."

Re-democratization and the politics of memory

Today Argentina stands out for the degree of visibility and sophistication of memory debates. There are several reasons for this, but one of the most important is the comparatively weakened credibility of the country's armed forces in the 1983 transition from dictatorship, given the military's disastrous handling of the economy, defeat in the Falklands war, and notoriety for the level and scope of human rights abuse under the dictatorship. This allowed more public space for the post-authoritarian regime to implement policies that included a trial of the military juntas, state-sponsored investigation of the abuses, and compensation for victims. Such activity at the level of formal political institutions helped foster a wide-ranging level of debate on memories and their representations.

Yet the road toward human rights successes and the art of commemoration was volatile. Both during and after the precedent-setting trials of the former military junta leaders in 1985, the Raúl Alfonsín government (1983–89) faced small-scale military rebellions from officers protesting military budget reductions, forced retirements of generals, and continued prosecutions of the many military officials implicated in the human rights violations. Argentines massively condemned the military rebellions, urging the government to stay the course. Nevertheless, in 1986 and 1987, Alfonsín implemented legislation that both put a deadline on court case filings by the families of the victims (known as the Full Stop law) and protected officers who could claim they were following orders (known as the Due Obedience law).

In addition to the military's relentless efforts to re-establish its authority and to avoid prosecution, economic instability plagued Alfonsín's administration, and many analysts and advisers counseled the need to "turn the page" on the past in order to address inflation, unemployment, and fiscal crisis. In fact, much of the mainstream academic wisdom of the 1980s asserted that the lesson of Argentina's ambitious human rights policies—trials and convictions of the generals, continued investigations and prosecutions of other human rights violators, and compensation for the victims—were too costly for a re-democratizing regime facing a host of political, social, and economic challenges. In 1989, Alfonsín left the presidency a year early, amidst continued military rebellions and economic crisis.

Shortly after assuming office, the new Argentine president Carlos Menem (1989–99) struck a deal with the military that decreed pardons for all those who had been convicted in return for an end to military uprisings. It was a severe blow to human rights victims. Yet the human rights movement, other influential civil society groups, and key members of the judiciary refused to accept the constitutionality of closing the books on human rights criminality under the dictatorship. Through the 1990s, human rights groups, journalists, and judges focused on crimes excluded from the Due Obedience law, particularly those involving abductions of children of the disappeared, to press for new convictions. By 2000, four of the formerly pardoned junta leaders and dozens of lower ranking officers had been charged and imprisoned for child kidnapping and illegal adoption. In 2005, first the Argentine Congress and Senate and then the Argentine Supreme Court revoked the previous laws that had protected the military from prosecution for violations. This allowed major trials of the former human rights violators to resume and continue throughout the country.

Carlos Nino, the late Argentine legal theorist and chief architect of human rights policies prior to Alfonsín's reversals, claimed that prosecutions of past perpetrators strengthened "the moral consciousness of society . . . [to] help overcome the corporatism, anomie, and concentration of power that all too long have been hallmarks of Argentine society."[13] While Nino recognized the Argentine process as imperfect, such imperfections, he argued, came from an administration that had attempted to conduct a truth and accountability process precisely within the letter of the law, to reinforce the legitimacy of the historic Argentine constitution.

Nino's emphasis on re-establishing a constitutional democratic legal framework, ethically validated by broad sectors of Argentine society, also captured the tenor of memory debates from the mid-1980s to the mid-1990s. A clean break from the dictatorial past and from the denial of basic civil liberties had to be established, and the demand for justice meant holding perpetrators legally accountable. Those who were murdered and disappeared were remembered as victims of horrendous criminal intent and needed to be understood as such. The effort focused on retrieving and verifying the painful details of the violations and on asserting such truths in the face of a volatile economy, a military institution arguing that it was battling a war against subversion, and an atmosphere of doubt regarding where post-authoritarian regime priorities should lie. The political aspects and intents of the victims awaited further explication.

The Argentine military continued to insist as it had under the dictatorship, that the armed forces were fighting a "Dirty War," and that those who died in this war were unpatriotic subversives. This war memory narrative suggests there were two more or less equivalent sides. Through the 1980s and 1990s, the notion of a dirty war dominated Argentine discourse on the past. Moreover, the official justification for the military *coup d'état* and the repression to follow was to end the chaos caused by the "two demons," the extreme right and the extreme left. As Marguerite Feitlowitz argued, the authoritarian regime crafted an entire lexicon to rationalize its rule, a lexicon whose resonance continued into Argentina's *Nunca Más* truth commission report and into a wider range of battles over memory.[14]

In fact, this contrived narrative deliberately overlooked the massive and violent military rout of the Argentine left. From 1976 on, among the 9,000–30,000 Argentines killed and disappeared, the tens of thousands of exiles and "insiles,"[15] and the many thousands who were imprisoned but survived, the majority were clearly not in the guerrilla movement, whose organizations were wiped out, both at home and abroad, well before the end of the dictatorship.

In addition, paralleling the pattern of societal claims in post-apartheid South Africa and post-fascist Germany, Argentine society shut its eyes to the atrocities committed during the dictatorship. Most prisons were clandestine, the practice of disappearance left little evidence, and the press and media were heavily censored. The *Nunca Más* truth commission report became an instant bestseller, as Argentines began to acknowledge the brutality of the dictatorship. In fact, in her study of Argentines born during or in the immediate aftermath of the military regime, and echoing similar attitudes among Chileans discussed in the previous chapter, Susana Kaiser argues that the silences regarding the past in Argentina, coupled with the dominant presentation of that past as a dirty war, contributed to young people's and others' suspicions about those who were killed as having done something wrong.[16]

As a consequence, even though Argentina was far better poised to hold its military human rights violators accountable than the more powerful and less unpopular militaries of Chile or Peru, Argentine human rights organizations proved constantly on the defensive. This is not to say that the Argentine guerrillas were peace loving and democratic, and debates about the nature, tactics, ideologies, and objectives of the urban guerrilla movement, including their role in the political instability of the early 1970s and the decisions that cost many their lives, represent another important set of memory debates today. Exploring political activism, political resistance, or those who joined the urban guerrilla movement in the context of the 1960s and 1970s entered dangerous discursive ground.[17]

In tandem with the memory debates, artists were integral to grassroots Argentine efforts to ensure that the new government not renege on its promise to seek truth and justice for the disappeared. In 1983, in the early days of transition from the military to a democratically elected regime, white silhouettes of human figures appeared all over Buenos Aires. Conceived by artists and in conjunction with the internationally known Mothers of the Plaza de Mayo, the *Siluetazo* drew thousands of participants into the making and mounting of life-sized silhouettes, and "the streets and squares of Buenos Aires were spontaneously transformed into a giant collective, open-air workshop."[18] Well after the commemorative act, the ghost-like silhouettes haunted the city streets. They appeared, faded, and reappeared through the 1980s.

Agency and memory

Nevertheless, memory debates would not tackle the Argentine military's "unpatriotic subversives" charge against those who were killed and disappeared until the mid-1990s. Argentine literary scholar María Sondereguer argues that open discussion regarding the nature and meaning of the guerrilla movements of the 1970s came in 1996, on the twentieth anniversary of the military *coup d'état*.[19] Timed with the anniversary, the release of a documentary that featured interviews with former Montonero militants played a dominant role in the debate, and a prominent left newspaper invited contributions from younger and older journalists, intellectuals, and former revolutionary leaders to reflect on the Montoneros. The essayists took quite distinct positions and tones, opening space to debate the meanings of revolutionary leadership and militancy, the relationship between older and younger generations of the left, and the context of the times then and now. The contributors also raised the question of who comprises the "we" when it comes to understanding who sacrificed, who lost, or who made costly errors in judgment.[20] Sondereguer marks this as the beginning of important critical dialogues that allow Argentines to delve into the politics of the revolutionary left in ways that were previously too difficult or painful.

Great tension also surrounds the emotionally difficult issue of surviving militants when so many of their comrades are dead and missing. Some, like Traverso, survived by escaping arrest altogether, while others survived their time in prison. In her study of several novels on the guerrilla movement, cultural critic Ana Longoni focuses our attention on these themes of survivor guilt and betrayal. She claims that ex-guerrilla survivors, particularly those who were imprisoned but survived, are forced to live with a kind of double punishment:

> [ex-political prisoners are both] victims of their captors and condemned by their old political organizations.
>   The conception that prevailed in the armed organizations was that death was better than betrayal, or of even running the risk of involuntary betrayal . . . To be taken prisoner alive was not so much a mistake as one's own fault, even a crime.[21]

But was it really a choice the imprisoned could make? Longoni emphasizes that ultimately it was the torturers, those who detained and held militants, who determined who would live and who would be killed. Yet the working through of the pain, loss, and guilt, in part through comparatively more open discussion, spaces for commemoration, and in the context of new guilty sentences for former military repressors, continues to constitute a tremendous challenge.

Like the recent memory debates establishing the disappeared as political militants, Traverso's *bicis* politicize the disappeared as subjects of their destinies. He creates the bicycles to remember the men and women who resisted the state, who gave their lives not in service to the state, but in struggling against the dictatorship. At the same time, the bicycle riders never stood a chance. "Dirty" is quite a euphemism for disappearing young people on bikes. One of those who resisted and disappeared helped to save Traverso from the same fate. Traverso's *bicis* represent his own working through of this tragic personal loss. Traverso both recognizes he is fortunate to be alive and feels a sense of responsibility, even joy, to create works that remember his comrades and resonate among other individuals and collectivities at home and abroad.

As part of a broader societal debate, there is increasing attention in Argentina to the question of the pervasive civilian complicity with the military repression. Theorist Mahmood Mamdani provocatively asserts the question

Figure 5.3 Bici (photo by Katherine Jensen).

of who are the beneficiaries of genocide. In comparing the genocide of Rwanda with the apartheid system of South Africa, he argues that in Rwanda, there were many perpetrators of human rights crimes, and few beneficiaries, while in South Africa, there were few perpetrators of human rights crimes yet many beneficiaries of the system. The challenge for post-apartheid South Africa, then, is not just one of holding perpetrators accountable to victims, but of holding beneficiaries accountable to the structural violences against apartheid's many victims.[22] Some now argue publicly that the beneficiaries in Argentina are all who welcomed order and stability and failed to challenge, much less confront, the military's injustices.

Argentine artists continually challenge the claim, "We didn't know." In 1976, making ironic, premonition-like use of this assertion of ignorance as his title, internationally acclaimed Argentine artist León Ferrari first published *We Didn't Know*. The book was a compilation of articles Ferrari had clipped from major Argentine newspapers that year, reporting on the many dead bodies and on families' legal filings to seek information regarding their family members' imprisonment and disappearances.[23] After his return in 1983 from exile, Ferrari continued to use the clippings in his art montages, exhibited throughout the country and around the world.

In Rosario's Museum of Memory, there is a room that contains maps and locations of the former clandestine detention centers, driving home the enormity and pervasiveness of the centers. On one wall of the room are the words of Argentine scholar Pilar Calveiro: "For its physical proximity, in the middle of society, *on the other side of the wall*, the concentration camp can only exist in the midst of a society that chooses not to see."[24] Museum of Memory director Rubén Chababo makes a strong case for the historically embedded nature of Argentines' acceptance of the repression. Drawing from particular historical and conceptual strands in both Germany and Argentina, Chababo traces the parallels and urges Argentines and others to engage in some serious soul searching:

> The question for the Argentine case, then,—but also for all other similar cases in the history of the twentieth century—is why a human community prefers to deny what is evident to the eye, or along the same line, how do the mechanisms of denial work to make what is evident seem more opaque or blurred and to lead communities to consent to situations that contradict the most basic principles of the human condition? . . . The memory of the horror cannot work, in itself, as an antidote immunizing us against its happening again unless there is some sort of a deeper introspective work being done by this memory work that forces us to ask ourselves what our own responsibility was in terms of making such horror possible.[25]

Commemorative conflicts

From the outset of his term, Argentine President Nestor Kirchner (2003–07) embraced a platform of coming to terms with the atrocities of the past. Among several symbolic–discursive acts, Kirchner announced that a military training school, the Navy School of Mechanics (ESMA) in Buenos Aires, once a notorious center of torture and forced disappearance, would be converted into a museum of memory. Kirchner attempted to claim a moral high ground by championing measures to expose Argentina's painful past and hold its chief architects accountable. And to the surprise of many, Kirchner actually rewrote the prologue to *Nunca Más*. In 2006, on the thirtieth anniversary of the Argentine military coup, the Kirchner government reissued the official truth commission report, adding a new prologue. The original text reads, "During the 1970s, Argentina was convulsed by terror coming as much from the extreme right as the extreme left." In the new edition, the prologue states:

> It is important to firmly establish, because constructing the future requires sound foundations, that it is unacceptable to pretend to justify State terrorism as a result of a violent game among opposing sides as if it were possible to find a justificatory symmetry . . .[26]

The Kirchner government officially pronounced the "two demons" argument as an unacceptable rationale for the military coup and the state terrorism that ensued.

President Kirchner's announcement that the ESMA would be converted into a memory museum responded affirmatively to several years of intense lobbying from a range of human rights organizations. As part of the broader opening up of memory debates, leading human rights non-governmental Memoria Abierta director Patricia Valdez notes that there was a palpable shift among Argentine human rights groups that began in 1996, on the twentieth anniversary of the coup.[27] Human rights groups who since 1983 had focused on struggles to determine the whereabouts of loved ones and to hold persecutors accountable began increasingly to mobilize around activities oriented toward public memory, including memorials.

Yet intense debate arose over ESMA's significance. This began between human rights groups demanding ESMA be recognized for what it was, on the one hand, and different government administrations and branches of the military anxious to convert the center into something other than a memorial to the atrocities of the past. While the municipal government of the city of Buenos Aires proved sympathetic to establishing ESMA as a memory museum, as well as other memorials, the federal government was not so forthcoming.

Upon Kirchner's announcement, the battle over what to do with the ESMA shifted to one among the human rights organizations themselves. Internationally acclaimed Argentine artist Marcelo Brodsky spearheaded a major call for proposals for what to do with the space, published as *Memory Under Construction. Debating What to Do with the ESMA*. Brodsky elicited conceptual think pieces from well-known memory scholars, and he and his team put together an impressive range of provocative images and texts. He vetted artists whose work had focused on state repression and who presented their ideas for the art they deemed appropriate for the space. Human rights organizations submitted proposals that Brodsky republished as excerpts or in their entirety.

Memory under construction: The debate revealed real difference regarding uses of the space. Artistic proposals ranged from representational paintings and sculptural pieces on torture and death, to far more abstract renderings of loss. Artists proposed installations that re-created torture chambers, as well as collections of every day appliances, gadgets, keepsakes, books, and photos that intelligence agents stole from those they abducted.[28] Most human rights groups also proposed that at least part of the space be re-created as the clandestine torture and disappearance center that it was. Yet the faction of the Mothers of the Plaza de Mayo led by Hebe Bonafini insisted that the space be given to them to create a cultural center for shows, art exhibitions, and classes, that it not be used as a museum where "people would go one time to see all the horror and never see it again."[29]

Splits over what to do with the ESMA once again brought to the surface longstanding tensions among politicized human rights organizations. For several years, the weekly ritual of the renowned Mothers of the Plaza de Mayo silently circling the Plaza had in fact become two distinct factions. Until

Kirchner's election to the presidency, one group of mothers was seen as the more reformist group that felt negotiating with the government toward legal progress on finding their loved ones was the appropriate position, while the group of mothers led by Hebe Bonafini was viewed as the more radical, revolutionary group that refused compromise.

As president, Kirchner and the Bonafini group became close allies, and the administration granted major funding to Bonafini's Mothers of the Plaza de Mayo. This support effectively marginalized the other group, as well as several human rights organizations that lacked the resources to conduct the research, commemorative work, and educational outreach they had hoped would be forthcoming from the government.

On August 8, 2008, Bonafini demonstrated the kind of activity she wished to see take place in the ESMA space, inaugurating the new "Our Children Cultural Space." Bonafini began an "anti-capitalist" cooking class. Holding up a bag of rice before her students, Bonafini explained that the rice was grown by Monsanto, a "multinational monster of neoliberalism" that was ruining Argentina's agricultural production for local consumption. Bonafini's first class attracted fifty students (and the press).

Splits among human rights and other grassroots organizations are inevitable, especially in a country as rich as Argentina is in political and cultural discourse. Groups vie for scarce funding, take distinct political and ideological positions, and often tire of the constant fighting. In his writing about memory and Argentina, Andreas Huyssen has observed that commemorative artistic efforts, human rights NGOs, and the Mothers of the Plaza de Mayo should be understood as intricately interwoven and "ultimately depend on each other and reinforce each other in their diversity, even if the representatives of different groups do not see eye to eye on the politics of their respective enterprises."[30]

Memory Park's multiple iterations

In 2007, I learned of the tensions and break-ups over the design and implementation of Buenos Aires's Memory Park. This is a sculpture park underway since the late 1990s that had whittled down to the support of a fraction of the individuals and organizations that initially spearheaded the concept.

The visit came amidst a downpour of rain. I waited for my young tour guide in a restaurant, *Los Platitos*, across the street from the park. The people working in the restaurant were extremely friendly, and we began a conversation about the park. After a little while, the manager pulled out a handful of brochures the restaurant had produced: On the cover is a photograph of the restaurant with the claim, "A classy place located on the best part of Coastal Drive." Inside, the brochure features a large, colorful map of *Memory Park*, indicating where the current and future sculptures are or will be situated. Los Platitos published the brochure on the twenty-fifth anniversary of the coup, and the brochure says, "Twenty-five years ago, we remember. Today we construct our memory." Yet I gasped in disbelief when I read the bottom:

"Remember . . . What's right in front of you! Los Platitos Restaurant!" But Luz Rodríguez, my tour guide, told me that the restaurant workers were always friendly and supportive, that they often held the key to the entrance as a favor. She said the commission staff found the brochure comical.

Luz and I sat in the small trailer that served as a temporary office for the park. She recounted some of her experiences with tours and her confidence that the park would be near completion in a year. In the middle of our visit, a tour bus pulled up, and in walked fifty architecture students from the National University of Rosario. It took me a long time to get up the nerve to ask them if they knew of the *bicis*. They all did. Moreover, they claimed that everyone in Rosario knows what the *bicis* represent.

The students then told me that the *bicis* are in memory of a well-known Rosarino social activist, Pocho Leprati, who was killed during the protests of 2001. In fact, they said, León Gieco, a popular Argentine musician, had composed a song entitled, "The Angel of the *bicis*" to remember him. I would soon discover the great significance of this transposition of Traverso's subject.

I watched the students as they tried to make sense of the three sculptures installed in the park, particularly that of US artist William Tucker's twenty-two-foot sculpture of reinforced concrete, entitled "Victory." They were skeptical and many seemed unimpressed. Yet when Luz placed the sculpture into context, explaining the way it was constructed, pulled from the ground, resurrected in a sense, the students nodded more approvingly.[31] Many were visibly moved by Roberto Aizenberg's "Untitled," three abstract figures that represent young people the artist knew and loved who disappeared. And as architecture students, they understood the intent of Dennis Oppenheim's "Monument to Escape," boxed cells that represent both enclosure, imprisonment, and liberation, escape. Many students spent considerable time studying the hundreds of black-and-white photos of the disappeared that lined the temporary wall. The students took lots of pictures and then boarded the bus.

A year later, in July 2008, I returned to Memory Park, curious about the park's progress as well as whether there was much foot traffic through the space. To get to the park this time, I hopped in a taxi, asking first to pass by the ESMA, then to Memory Park. The driver knew the enormous ESMA, but he had never heard of "any memory park." He leaned out his cab window to consult another driver. The other driver had no idea, either. While I am not very good with directions, I did remember more or less where Memory Park was, along the River Plate, and we managed to find it. At the time I arrived, the Memory wall was fenced off, not open to the public, but I obtained permission to enter.

The foreground of the park had not changed since the previous year. The sculptures by Tucker, Aizenberg, and Oppenheim continued to be the only sculptures in the park. Yet now the central sculptural feature of the park had been built: the *Monument to the Victims of State Terrorism*. The wall divides the park from the river and is foregrounded by a large reflecting pool. Visitors walk along the wall in a gradual ascent that zigzags. The names of the dead and disappeared begin with the year 1969 and build to a physical crescendo in 1976 and 1977, ending in 1982. Beside each name is an age—18, 19, 21— these seemed to be the most common, or at least the ages that gave me pause. Beside several of the names and ages was also the word, "*embarazada*," (pregnant). There are almost 10,000 names.

Construction workers were on site continuing to build the documentation center and to pave the surrounding grounds. The trailer where Luz and I met the year before continued to serve as the park's office, and on the day I visited, another young woman had taken Luz's place. It was difficult to gauge how much Memory Park was visited now, though the young woman assured me that visitors were fairly frequent.

Since my 2008 visit, Memory Park has further transformed. The wall is complete, as is a major documentation center. There are several new sculptures, including Marie Orensanz's "To Think is a Revolutionary Act," Nicolás Guagnini's "30,000," and Claudia Fontes's river piece, "Reconstruction of the Portrait of Pablo Míguez." The Argentine art collective, the *Grupo de Arte Callejero*, has installed "Signs of Memory," a pathway of signage that contextualizes and maps distinct dimensions of the repressive period. According to the three university students serving as guides at the information office (still the small trailer) during my visit in December 2010, there were more than 10,000 visitors over that year. The number largely represents elementary and high school groups. The visit to Memory Park served as an important reminder that commemorative spaces are ongoing processes that, much like the Río de la Plata, haunt and inspire, ebb and flow.

Collaboration toward global connection

Fernando Traverso's choice of a bicycle stencil is rooted in his memory of a disappeared comrade, "Cachilo," for whom Traverso stenciled *bici* number 350. Traverso described how as a part of the resistance to the dictatorship, they worked in a poor Rosarino neighborhood together, helping to provide basic needs to families there. Cachilo knew Traverso as "Bicho." Traverso described Cachilo as very special, as someone who was very active and who connected various members of the resistance together. Cachilo and Bicho would talk about what was happening around them, about their political convictions as Montoneros, and about why they did not leave the resistance. They concluded that they could not stop because it would be a betrayal of the comrades before them who had fallen.

Cachilo always rode an old English black bike that his uncle had given him, a "relic even during those days," Traverso said. The last time they were to meet, Cachilo signaled to Traverso though his eyes and his movements that something was wrong, that he and Bicho should not talk, that they should keep moving past one another. Traverso understood. That evening Traverso saw Cachilo's *bici* leaning against a tree. Several days later, it was still there.

Figure 5.4 Fernando Traverso (photo by Katherine Hite).

More than twenty years later, Traverso's deep pain and the need to relieve the pain led to his creation of a *bici*. On March 24, 2001, the twenty-fifth anniversary of the military *coup d'état*, Traverso stenciled the *bici* alone in the cover of night. Traverso soon honed the *bici*-making process, designing a lighter, easy-to-carry three-piece stencil rather than the original two-piece stencil. Traverso numbered and photographed each of the *bicis*, finding a good deal of internal joy in returning to find them the day after he stenciled them. After stenciling and documenting the first several *bicis*, Traverso recruited close friends to collaborate, including former comrades from their days in the resistance and from his years of internal exile in the city of Saladas, in the province of Corrientes.

In an interview in 2004 with memory museum director Rubén Chababo, Traverso said that in the process of creating the *bicis* on Rosario's walls, he discovered how their presence became virtual personifications:

[The *bici* were] physically at the limits of the corporeal and the intangible, they were opening the sense of different stories and interrogations for everyone who saw them. I could confirm that they produced a real interruption in people's daily walks, they invited those who saw them to ask themselves about where they came from and the reason behind their enigmatic appearance: Who left that bicycle? Who is or was its owner? What interrupted its trip? Who was it waiting for who was detained?[32]

Traverso told Chababo that he was already accustomed to the telephone ringing and his being asked to stencil the bike's image in a particular site, on the front of a family's home, on the wall of a factory, and already in 2004, requests were coming in from other cities, from people who had come through Rosario, learned of the *bicis*, and wanted to place them in their own landscapes.[33]

Traverso and his artist collective, "The Worker–Student Coordinating Committee," create graffiti art throughout Rosario, primarily to commemorate historic workers struggles and more contemporary struggles against neo-liberalism, police brutality and unjust incarceration. I came to recognize their distinctive commemorative graffiti work throughout the city, including an image of a television set (depicted on the jacket cover) to symbolize the Argentine government's declaration of a state of siege during the 2001 protests.

Traverso was also a co-founder of the Rosario artist collective, Grupo En Trámite, which collaborated for several years. As described in the introductory chapter, on March 24, 2000, the twenty-fourth anniversary of the Argentine coup, En Trámite launched its first major public art installation, *Descongesta*. The piece was composed of old pairs of shoes embedded in forty blocks of ice. The artists placed the piece on a corner in front of the former center for clandestine detention and torture that was converted into a fancy bar, called Rock and Fellers. As the ice blocks melted in the hot sun, the ice formed pools of water on the sidewalk and then evaporated altogether, leaving the shoes sprawled along the pavement. "Nothing more inoffensive than a puddle on the sidewalk," the artists claimed. "A flash of memory to anesthetize the coldness of forgetting, to chill the pain."[34] En Trámite repeated the installation later that year. While En Trámite no longer exists, Traverso has found new energy with other artist–activist collectives. The groups gather to plan and carry out creative artistic actions at protests, press conferences, and commemorative dates.

During my return to Rosario in December 2010 for the inauguration of the Museum of Memory, I talked with Traverso about the new museum space. For the artist, the museum is too much of a high culture display, the politics emptied from the scenario. Traverso was concerned that the museum is too "first world."[35] I appreciated this concern, though I suggested that perhaps there was room for distinct memory efforts, including this one, designed to reach new publics. Traverso agreed that this might be the case, but he worried about which memory efforts would dominate and which might recede to the shadows.

On February 22, 2011, Traverso's collective paid tribute to Oscar Bouvier, a twenty-one-year-old Montonero militant of Rosario who disappeared in September 1976 and whose remains were discovered in November 2010. Titled, "A star for *el Gusi*," the commemorative piece was a star of ice, dyed with red food coloring, and as the star melted, the water formed liked pools of blood.

New generations of artist collectives have emerged throughout the country, including the Erroristas, Etcetera, and Arte Callejera. Marcelo Brodsky sees these new generations emanating from the street mobilizations in the midst of the Argentine economic crisis of 2001–02.[36] The artist collectives participate in a range of actions, bringing creative visual expression to AIDS awareness, *escraches*, workers' strikes, unemployed picketers.

Together on Traverso's roof we laid out the stencil of the *bici* over a piece of canvas and spray-painted a *bici* for me. In return, I committed to find the *bici* an appropriate home and photograph it and send the photograph to Traverso to include with hundreds of others on his website. It is another way in which he is a complete collaborationist, an artist contributing to a truly global imaginary. While I have not found a permanent home for the canvas, I shared it with my seminar students as we discussed Traverso's work, and we gathered around the stenciled image to take a photograph, which we sent to Traverso.

In Rosario, the *bicis* took on new significance. When Traverso's first *bici* appeared, Argentina had been thrown into the global crisis perpetrated by the IMF and World Bank's neoliberal policies. Like other cities of the interior, Rosario was hit particularly hard. The city struck back. Protests against the banks, and against the IMF and World Bank, became intense and numerous.

One of Rosario's grassroots social movement organizers was Pocho Leprati, by many accounts a loved, handsome, poor, almost Christ-like figure. The accounts of how Leprati died vary somewhat among Rosarinos. Many told me he was shot by police during a protest, as Leprati tried to warn the police that children were inside the building the police were about to raid. Others told me Pocho was shot on his *bici* as he rode to an organizing meeting. As the Rosarino architecture students affirmed during their and my 2007 visit to Memory Park in Buenos Aires, Traverso's *bicis* have transcended the commemoration of young leftists of the twentieth century to commemorate their own twenty-first-century martyr.

Popular accounts of the death of Leprati are similar to accounts of the death of Luigi Trastulli, a militant who died during an Italian workers strike in Turin many decades ago. Renowned oral historian Alessandro Portelli contrasts popular memories of Trastulli's death with the accounts according to police, newspapers, and the coroner's office.[37] Portelli argues that the people of Turin needed to remember Trastulli as a martyr, to champion him in the midst of a terrible crisis, in which ordinary people felt quite powerless and desperate. The "validity," the "truth," Portelli argues, is far less important than the ways people remember their pasts in order to affirm their lives' meanings in the present. To remember Trastulli as a martyr of the Turin workers serves to empower, to transform tragedies into struggles for justice that his companions seek hard to embrace. So, too, is the death of Leprati, who Rosarinos now remember when they see the *bicis* in their streets. In fact, the death of Leprati has already transcended the boundaries of Rosario. The *bicis* have come to be read as a struggle against social injustices, wrought by the neoliberal crisis internationally.

Figure 5.5 Stencil, Angel of the *bici* Pocho Leprati (photo by Katherine Jensen).

Traverso's *bicis* can now be found throughout the Americas and Europe—from Paraguay, to Colombia, El Salvador, Mexico, South Dakota, throughout Spain, and in eastern Europe as well. The images of the *bicis* on Fernando's website convey a vast array of meanings. For many, the *bicis* clearly remember Argentines who have been lost. In Cali, Colombia, a group downloaded the *bici* as a statement about poverty. In Zaragosa, Spain, the *bici* was adopted by environmentalists to promote sustainable living. In the Basque Country of Spain, Basque nationalists used a stenciled *bici* to represent the plight of widows of the violence. These multiple meanings are also, as Michael Rotherberg emphasizes, multidirectional—local and globalized, past and present.[38] They establish connections among diverse communities that engage with one another virtually and on the ground. Perhaps because of his global travels, communication, and reach, Traverso has more recently developed a stencil of a small envelope, which he has termed a *carta*, or letter. The *cartas* are found "tucked" at the foot of a door, or near a sewer grate, or close to a mailbox. Like the *bicis*, Traverso's *cartas* are now beginning to find their ways into communities around the world.

The *bicis* as well constitute memory art *from* the border. In May 2009, Traverso traveled to the border cities of Ciudad Juárez, in the state of Chihuahua, Mexico, and to El Paso, Texas, USA, invited by student activist

Figure 5.6 Dress fabric stenciled with a *bici* (photo by Fernando Traverso).

Figure 5.7 University students of Juárez, Mexico stenciling dress fabric
(photo by Fernando Traverso).

Figure 5.8 Bici under a bridge leading to the Mexico–US border
(photo by Fernando Traverso).

groups to help them commemorate the femicide of several hundred young women. "I was working with two universities, one in Texas and the Autonomous University in Juárez," Traverso said.

> We used fabric that bore the same prints as the dresses of the women who have been killed (as illustrated in Figures 5.6 and 5.7). In addition to the prints, we used solid colors and white fabrics. We had one black fabric, which unfortunately served to protest the recent assassination of a professor. In the two cities *bicis* and *cartas* remain there.[39]

Juárez activists also stenciled a *bici* on a supporting wall of a bridge leading to the Mexico–US border. As the activists stenciled, a group of citizens of Juárez applauded the work, thinking that the bicycle symbolized a protest against the recent shutting down of the special bicycle lane many Mexicans who work in El Paso used to ride to work each morning. Traverso's *bicis* model memorials as gateways into conversations that thread the past to the present, into collective action that demands that viewers take notice.

Epilogue

In October 2010, flanked by state forensics officials and their lawyers, Paine, Chile family members confirmed the remains of nine of their loved ones. In the midst of planning for the funerals and burials, a delegation of family members met with Chilean bishop Juan Ignacio González to negotiate the purchase of a mausoleum in the Paine Cemetery. Bishop González, an Opus Dei priest and staunch supporter of the former dictatorship, objected to the families' request. González did not want one mausoleum representing the entire collective of Paine's dead and disappeared.[1] González said that he understood they had suffered, but that the families "on the other side" had also suffered.[2] After more than a month of lobbying the priest, including bringing in high-level government officials to force a change in his decision, bishop González relented.

The experience with the bishop was another grim reminder of the continuing political tensions over the past in Paine, and of the ways in which Paine families continue to relive traumatic memories. Much of the AFDD-Paine's work following the October 2010 funerals shifted to incorporating into the prosecution process those relatives who had not yet pressed charges. Fear, anxiety, a wish not to relive the pain, or the perceived and real lack of financial resources to pursue prosecutions prevented several Paine families from fully participating in the long legal road of demanding accountability for the murders of their loved ones. Divisions arose within the AFDD over how to balance efforts to reinvigorate prosecution procedures with the ongoing need to maintain the memorial.

And indeed, over the past several years the Chilean judiciary has steadily investigated and prosecuted hundreds of human rights crimes. As of September 2010, 777 military, police, and civilians had been prosecuted for crimes ranging from torture and illegal exhumation to kidnapping, execution and disappearance.[3] Of the 777, the majority awaited sentencing and convictions. Sixty-nine people were in prison. In the Paine case, eighteen people, including nine civilians, seven retired police officers, and two retired army officers, had been prosecuted as suspects. Army Brigadier General Victor Raúl Pinto Pérez was serving time as the author of multiple kidnappings and homicides, though as of this writing he had not been sentenced for his role in Paine. Lieutenant

Osvaldo Magaña and others continued to be free while awaiting sentencing. On July 26, 2010, retired police officer Luis Jara, who was prosecuted as a suspect in 2004 for his role in the Paine disappearances and executions, committed suicide.

The remains that were confirmed in October 2010 included no more than the eyeglasses and a piece of the pantleg of René Maureira, whose widow Sonia Carreño confirmed that they were her husband's. For grandson Juan René, the news was an unanticipated shock. He realized he had denied the idea that his grandfather would ever be found, and he viewed the search for this particular truth as more of a preoccupation of his elders. Now, some thirty-seven years after his grandfather's kidnapping and disappearance, Juan René joined his grandmother in a flood of feelings and speculations:

> It was very painful. On the one hand, we felt the accomplishment of having accessed the truth, through the materialization of my grandfather's glasses. Yet on the other hand, our mood could hardly be understood as celebratory. You can't feel the happiness of this "conquest." It might be different in other areas, like the happiness we could feel in having won a meeting space at the *Paine Memorial*. We could say, "This is a conquest, we can celebrate it, we accomplished something." In the case of finding the remains of our loved ones, the feelings are complex, you can't feel like celebrating, like feeling happy, and I finally understood what my grandmother had experienced for so much of her life. You begin to take on the loss, and not only the loss, but the magnitude of the tragedy as well. Seeing my grandfather's glasses, it was like, on the one hand we now had a part of him, those glasses had held up for so many years, but on the other hand, it really made me imagine what happened to him that night—how he might have died, really, and I asked myself whether the glasses fell off his head when they assassinated him . . . My grandmother wants to keep the glasses to show people what she calls "the footprint of the crime," to show that this is what they did.[4]

At the same time that the Paine families were facing the atrocities committed against their loved ones anew, in neighboring Argentina a similar process was underway. On October 23, 2010, thirty-four years after his disappearance in Argentina, Montonero militant Roberto De Vicenzo was laid to rest in Rosario. Earlier in the year, De Vicenzo's remains were discovered in an anonymous grave in a cemetery in Barrancas, some forty miles from Rosario. More than a hundred gathered at the funeral, and De Vincenzo was buried beside his wife Miriam Moro, also a Montonero militant, whose remains had been discovered in 1983.

As I read the article on the funeral in Rosario, I was struck by the parallels between the remarks of De Vicenzo's son Gustavo, thirty-four, and those of grandson Juan René Maureira, twenty-four, of Chile. The two men were burying their loved ones, who had been missing for well over thirty years, within a week of one another. I realized that at this moment, in each of the countries I was studying—Spain, Peru, Chile, and Argentina—there were families undergoing the traumas of exhumation and proper burials, no matter how distant the atrocities, all at the same time. And in each of the sites, the commemorative acts possessed a clear politics of the present—an expression of grief and mourning, but also a denunciation of the criminality of the deaths and a demand for accountability.

Just as memorials and commemorative political acts have exploded through-out Latin America and Spain, so, too, has the proliferation of "museums of memory," officially sponsored museums that convey the traumatic political pasts to a broad public. On December 17, 2010, the city of Rosario inaugurated its national Museum of Memory. As described in the previous chapter, the Museum represents the culmination of the city's decade-long effort to center the memory of state terrorism in Argentina, toward a "*nunca más,*" as well as toward the need to connect the human rights violations of the past with the struggle against ongoing violations.

The Rosario museum is designed with the utmost sophistication, benefitting from artistic talent, decades of painstaking research, a designer's eye, and deep respect for those who are missing, those who died and those who have survived. Each exhibit captures relationships between past and present, the local and the global, and between viewers as detached and viewers as responsible, even implicated.

Its inauguration emphasized inclusion of the citizens of Rosario, with two short but emotional speeches and an outdoor evening festival of music and art. The crowd gasped approvingly at the enormous visual montages projected directly and perfectly onto the museum's outer wall, and the audience frequently erupted in applause, singing along with well-known musicians performing songs of loss and struggle. The ceremony was a melding of sadness and joy, a celebration that the Museum had emerged victorious when it was not always so apparent this would be so. It represented an appreciation of cultural accomplishment, love, and pride.

While the selection of songs came from a mournful past, the com-memorative ceremony also emphasized ways the museum tied the past to the present. The museum announced a new human rights award in memory of the Rosarino activist, the "angel of the *bici*" Pocho Leprati, and the first awards went to a women's rights group and to a gay rights advocacy group. Standing beside the young women accepting the award was Methodist bishop Federico Pagura, a member of the Museum's directorate, who did not shrink when the spokeswoman for the group made a call for greater rights to an abortion, a call met with loud applause. Similarly, the bishop embraced the gay advocate as he discussed advances in gay marriage legislation and in the legal recognition of transgendered identities.

The morning after the museum inauguration I sat down with the artist of the *bicis* Fernando Traverso, who had also attended the opening ceremony and stood with the multitude outside. We talked about the events and commemorations in which Traverso had participated in the last year, both in Rosario and in Bogotá, Colombia, where he met vibrant human rights and political party militants from throughout Latin America. The many groups participated in alliance-building workshops and shared their creative cultural projects. One afternoon, organizations of families of the disappeared from Colombia, Peru, and El Salvador joined Traverso in a *bici* stenciling workshop out on the lawn to remember their loved ones.[5] Traverso felt such transcontinental human connection, one of anger and sadness over lost loved ones and the violences of power, yet also of mutual recognition, knowing, and solidarity.

In Lima, Peru, plans also advance, albeit fitfully, for a Museum of Memory. The proposed centerpiece for the museum is the collection of photographs that accompany the Peruvian Truth and Reconciliation Commission report. The photographs, which once inspired sculptor Lika Mutal to create *The Eye that Cries*, are now displayed in Lima's Museum of the Nation and have attracted thousands of visitors. Reproductions of the photographs have traveled to museums and institutions around the world. There is also discussion of moving *The Eye that Cries* memorial to grounds outside the future Museum of Memory, though given the attacks and controversy surrounding the memorial's brief history, there is no agreement on such a move.

On September 13, 2010, appointed Museum of Memory commissioner Mario Vargas Llosa resigned his position to protest Peruvian president Alan García's declaring an amnesty for human rights violators, members of the Peruvian military. While President García then rescinded the amnesty, Vargas Llosa refused to return as head of the museum.

Mutal told me that as of November 2010, approximately 10,000 names had been permanently engraved onto *The Eye that Cries* stones, names drawn from the list of the government's national reparations commission as they are publicly released.[6] On December 31, 2010, Peru's official Council on Reparations published more than 21,000 names of those who were killed and disappeared during the conflict and whose families merit compensation. The Council stated that its work documenting those citizens and families who should receive reparations would continue for another six months in provinces throughout the country.[7] During an August 28, 2010, ceremony at *The Eye that Cries* marking the anniversary of the Peruvian Truth and Reconciliation report, family members placed the recently engraved stones back on the memorial's labyrinth path.

In Spain, only the Spanish senate's conservative oppositional party, the Partido Popular, refused to support the September 2010 vote to insist that the government convert the *Valley of the Fallen* into a historic site that remembers all the fallen in the Civil War and in Franco's repression. Of the sites around the world that are being converted from one narrative of remembrance to another, the *Valley of the Fallen* certainly poses a formidable challenge.

To date, it is unclear how the conversion will take shape. Meanwhile, the stories of exhumations of those executed during the Spanish Civil War and in the early years of the Franco regime appear with greater frequency.

Moreover, the Spanish magistrate responsible for securing General Augusto Pinochet's 1998 arrest in London, judge Baltazar Garzón, faces charges leveled by right-wing political organizations sympathetic to the Franco regime. They have mounted a legal attack against Garzón to stop the magistrate's persistent attempts to prosecute human rights criminals of the Franco era.

In May 2010, I participated in a small conference on memorials held at the Mémorial de Caen in Caen, France. Culture and politics of memory experts on East Asia, Europe, Latin America, and the US gathered for what seemed to be an attempt to influence plans for the 9/11 Museum at New York City's Ground Zero, due to open September 11, 2012. New York City's *9/11 Memorial* and Museum was a co-sponsor of the conference, and Museum director Alice Greenwald and close adviser Clifford Chanin were both active participants. Over three days, each of us presented studies of commemorative processes and sites. Historian of Japan Carol Gluck emphasized Japan's moving away from nationalist commemorative practice as a gradual acknowledgment of the country's past imperialist violence. US cultural theorist Marita Sturken cautioned against commemoration as re-enactment and critiqued silences around the genealogies of violence.[8] Argentine architect Gonzalo Conte presented newly designed Argentine memory landscapes that invited open interpretation. In both implicit and explicit ways, several of us urged a 9/11 World Trade Center museum design that invited global reflection and mourning.

On the final day of the conference, Greenwald and Chanin presented plans for the 9/11 museum that flew in the face of any attempt to project an inclusive global imaginary. There was something so oddly paradoxical about the plans. On the one hand, the presenters claimed that September 11, 2001, was the most mediatized atrocity in world history, that in the course of twenty-four hours, an estimated two billion people around the globe are believed to have witnessed or watched the event. In addition, Greenwald and Chanin estimated that once it opened, roughly 500,000 international and US visitors would pass through the 9/11 museum each year. Yet the 9/11 museum design asserts an extreme nationalist narrative, focusing on America under attack, emphasizing shock value, evading context, and downplaying the loss of life of non-US as well as US citizens.

The design centers first and foremost on a re-enactment of events of the day, including the sunny, peaceful warmth of that fall morning, the dramatic appearance seemingly out of nowhere of the plane flying into the Twin Towers (as well as the planes that crashed into the Pentagon and in Shanksville, Pennsylvania), and the horror that followed. The display also features a moving series of images of the "first responders," the hundreds who rushed to assist in the rescue. The re-enactment conveys a "before the attack" as peaceful, and an "after the attack" as a heroic effort to take care of our own.

It was clear to me that what will most attract and repel visitors is one of the first museum exhibit features: Greenwald termed them the "protected audiovisual alcoves," that is, partially walled-off spaces for the more "difficult material," including recordings of frantic final cell phone calls to loved ones and video footage of those who jumped to their deaths from the high stories of the Twin Towers. I was mortified by the mere description of the alcoves, and the feeling never left me as Greenwald and Chanin continued with their presentation. My first thought was of a very close friend who lost another close friend in the World Trade Center attacks, and I could never imagine her setting foot in such a sensationalist display. One participant sitting next to me during the presentation called the re-enactment "pornographic."

The *9/11 Memorial* Museum displays move from the "difficult material" to a brief historical narrative that begins with the 1993 terrorist bombing of the World Trade Center, and then includes an excerpt from a speech of Osama bin Laden and tiny photographs of the nineteen terrorist airplane hijackers. The historical narrative felt designed chiefly to provoke visitors' anger at the attackers.

The entire design as it stood was such a missed opportunity. Citizens from ninety-two countries perished in the World Trade Center, yet a decision had been made only to present the names and faces of the 2,882 individuals, not to name the citizens' home countries. The decision was to focus squarely on America as the national innocent. While the *9/11 Memorial*—scheduled to open September 11, 2011, a full year before the museum opening and on the tenth anniversary of the tragedy—is a minimalist design and invites reflection, the Museum plays into Americans' worst tendencies to vilify, to hate the other. This will not go unnoticed.

In his visit to Vassar College, Rosario Museum of Memory curator Ruben Chababo discussed Argentines' fitful, difficult engagement with their country's atrocious past and then somewhat delicately challenged his primarily US audience:

> There is still a pending task in the academic curricula and an issue that has been silenced in public forums, and this is the degree of detachment with which processes of extreme violence are seen by communities and nations whose own governments have had an active role in bringing them about.[9]

In a November 2010–January 2011 exhibit entitled, "Winnipeg," at Chile's Museum of Memory, curators, academics, and activists mounted an installation of videos, photographs, and maps. The exhibit was named for the S.S. *Winnipeg*, a ship that carried more than 2,000 Spanish exiles in France at the end of the Spanish Civil War, landing on Chile's shores on September 3, 1939. Chilean ambassador to France Pablo Neruda arranged for the ship, which was greeted in the port of Valparaíso by Chilean health minister Salvador Allende. The exhibit features stories of the exiles told by their descendants, including

Chileans, Argentines, Uruguayans, and other Latin Americans. Decades later, some of the same descendants re-crossed the Atlantic in the 1970s as exiles to Spain. And the grandchildren and great-grandchildren of the Spanish Republicans and other Spanish exiles would cross the Atlantic once more, now as Europeans, as Latin America re-democratized in the 1980s and 1990s. The exhibit commemorates trans-Atlantic human connections and shared experiences of violence, causalities, sufferings, and solidarities across time and space.

Memorials can seek compassion, a connection between those who have lost and those who can feel this loss and be moved. Memorial forms, stagings, and sites are vessels for the multiplicity of representations, where individual and collective subjectivity can enter into dialogue with Otherness to help process and represent meaning. They invite respectful, often profound, engagement.

Memorialization, as we have seen, can embrace praxis. While the form of the memorial can provoke or invite, the actual taking up of the invitation requires human agency manifested in various and typically unforeseen ways. Distinct collectivities humanize and re-politicize the victims, at points producing, as in *The Eye that Cries*, a polarizing, angry, and very much alive conversation about who is a victim, who is a perpetrator. In an accordion-like fashion, the conversations can spiral out from museums and memorial sites, across communities, across borders. As the globalization of the reception of the *bicis* illustrates, shared global mourning over the universality of oppression can produce a politics that creates greater awareness and enjoins the viewers as participants in a broader social justice project.

Around the world, memorials themselves have become battlegrounds, as artists, designers, states, and societies negotiate how to convey, or evoke, or even shock, passersby into contemplation and reaction. Memorial conceptualizers have come to appreciate the unknowable dimension of just how deeply a monument will be perceived and by whom, as well as how perceptions of the memorial will change over time, in distinct political–historical moments. While memorials commemorate the past, they are inevitably also understood through lenses of the present. Memorials that represent past injustices invite those who mourn and those who contemplate the injustices to question what has changed, what has not changed, and what must change.

Notes

1 Memorials to struggle

1 For a synthetic reflection on conceptualizing memory, and memory's relation to politics in Latin America's Southern Cone, particularly, see Elizabeth Jelin, *State Repression and the Labors of Memory*, Minneapolis, MN: University of Minnesota Press, 2003.

2 Jan Assmann, "Collective Memory and Cultural Identity," *New German Critique*, 65, Cultural History/Cultural Studies, Spring-Summer, 1995, pp. 125–133. For a review of the founding sociological literature on memory, see Jeffrey K. Olick and Joyce Robins, "Social Memory Studies: From 'Collective Memory' to the Historical Sociology of Mnemonic Practices," *Annual Review of Sociology*, 24, 1998, pp. 105–140.

3 See, for example, Carol Mason, *Killing for Life: The Apocalyptic Narrative of Pro-Life Politics*, Ithaca, NY: Cornell University Press, 2002.

4 For a devastating account of the psychological state of returning GIs, see Jennifer Senior, "The Prozac, Paxil, Zoloft, Wellbutrin, Celexa, Effexor, Valium, Klonopin, Ativan, Restoril, Xanax, Adderall, Ritalin, Haldol, Risperdal, Seroquel, Ambien, Lunesta, Elavil, Trazodone War," *New York*, February 14, 2011, pp. 26–30, 83–84.

5 For a political theoretical effort to locate the unmoorings, see Wendy Brown, *Politics Out of History*, Princeton, NJ: Princeton University Press, 2001. For a discussion of the ways symbolic representations of nostalgia emerge in the context of major transition and uncertainty, see Maria Ferretti, "Nostalgia for communism in post-Soviet Russia," unpublished paper.

6 Pierre Nora, "Between Memory and History: *Les Lieux de Mémoire*," *Representations*, 26, Spring 1989.

7 Joan Didion, *The Year of Magical Thinking*, New York: Vintage International edition, 2007, p. 189.

8 Nevertheless, Didion's memoir of her struggle with the death of her husband is all the more haunting when I later learned, not through Didion's account, that Didion's daughter also died. Her memoir, then, is a testimony to her own profound denial.

9 Judith Butler, *Precarious Life: The Powers of Mourning and Violence*, London: Verso Books, 2004, pp. 19–49.

10 Butler, pp. 44, 32.

11 Diana Taylor, *Disappearing Acts: Spectacles of Gender and Nationalism in Argentina's "Dirty War,"* Durham, NC: Duke University Press, 1997.

12 For a clear argument of how this was done in Germany and elsewhere following World War I, see George L. Mosse, *Fallen Soldiers: Reshaping the Memory of the World Wars*, New York: Oxford University Press, 1990.

13 On our masterful use of euphemisms to mask war's destruction, see Elaine Scarry, *The Body in Pain: The Making and Unmaking of the World*, New York: Oxford University Press, 1985, particularly pp. 60–91.

14 For a discussion of state representations as violent erasures, see Jenny Edkins, *Trauma and the Memory of Politics*, Cambridge, UK: Cambridge University Press, 2003.

15 On the term "indexical," see Margaret Olin's discussion of Roland Barthes's theorizing photographs as memorials, "The Winter Garden and Virtual Heaven," in Robert S. Nelson and Margaret Olin, *Monuments and Memory, Made and Unmade*, Chicago: University of Chicago Press, 2003, p. 134.

16 Taylor, *Disappearing Acts*, p. 145.

17 Susan Sontag, *Regarding the Pain of Others*, New York: Picador, 2003, pp. 85–86.

18 Jelin, *State Repression and the Labors of Memory*, p. 20.

19 Pierre Nora laments this loss of patrimonial authority, this "transmission and conservation of collectively remembered values," as he documents the proliferation and pluralization of memory claims. See his "Between Memory and History: Les Lieux de Mémoire," *Representations*, 26, Spring 1989, p. 7.

20 For a description of the memorial project, see www.afsc.org/eyes/ (accessed July 18, 2008).

21 For a description of *Arlington West*, see www.arlingtonwestsantamonica.org/ (accessed July 18, 2008).

22 For a description of the Peace Ribbon Project, see www.codepink4peace.org/ section.php?id=17 (accessed November 1, 2010).

23 For a thoughtful discussion of the contradictory, ever-in-motion interpretations of collective projects such as these, see Marita Sturken, *Tangled Memories: The Vietnam War, the AIDS Epidemic, and the Politics of Remembering*, Berkeley: University of California Press, 1997, particularly pp. 216–217 on the AIDS quilt.

24 Interviews between the author and family members, July 2007 and May 2009.

25 Edkins, *Trauma and the Memory of Politics*, p. 15.

26 Anthropologist Alfred Gell has argued that this transformative character holds true of art. See his *Art and Agency: An Anthroplogical Theory*, Oxford: Oxford University Press, 1998.

27 Cited in Edkins, *Trauma and the Memory of Politics*, p. 5.

28 Arthur Danto, "The Vietnam Veterans Memorial," *The Nation*. August 31, 1986, p. 152. Cited in James E. Young, *The Texture of Memory: Holocaust Memorials and Meaning*, New Haven, CT: Yale University Press, 1993, p. 3.

29 Marita Sturken and James E. Young, "Monuments," *Encyclopedia of Aesthetics*, Volume 3, Oxford: Oxford University Press, 1998, pp. 272–287.

30 See Marita Sturken, "The Wall, the Screen, and the Image: The Vietnam Veterans Memorial," *Representations*, 35, 1991, pp. 118–142.

31 Kristin Ann Hass, *Carried to the Wall: American Memory and the Vietnam Veterans Memorial*, Berkeley, CA: University of California Press, 1998.

32 For an analysis of the fitful process of establishing the memorial wall and the memorial park of Buenos Aires, see Patricia Valdez, "El Parque de la Memoria en Buenos Aires," in Elizabeth Jelin and Victoria Langland, Eds., *Monumentos, memoriales y marcas territoriales*, Buenos Aires and Madrid: Siglo XXI, 2003, pp. 97–112.

33 Huyssen, Andreas, "Memory Sites in an Expanded Field: The Memory Park in Buenos Aires," in his *Present Pasts: Urban Palimpsests and the Politics of Memory*, Stanford, CA: Stanford University Press, 2003, p. 101.

34 Huyssen, *Present Pasts*, p. 103.

35 I thank former Vassar students Katie Jensen and Emily Thompson, class of 2009, for sharing their reflections and their photographs of Memory Park and the 2007 inauguration.

36 In an interview with government officials at the Ministry of Public Works I later learned that the original site for *Women in Memory* was to have been a pedestrian thoroughfare in downtown Santiago, but that members of the Chilean military objected, as it was also in front of residential buildings housing many retired military officers.

37 On continuities and changes in commemorative inscriptions and naming, see Daniel J. Sherman, "Bodies and Names: The Emergence of Commemoration in Interwar France," *American Historical Review*, April 1998, pp. 443–466.

38 Nora, "Between Memory and History: *Les Lieux de Mémoire*."

39 James Young, "Memory Against Itself in Germany Today: Jochen Gerz's Counter-monuments," in his *At Memory's Edge: After-Images of the Holocaust in Contemporary Art and Architecture*, New Haven, CT: Yale University Press, 2000, pp. 120–151. For an analysis of the broader counter-monument movement, including artists Gerz, Horst Hoheisel, Sol Lewitt, and others, see his "The Counter-Monument: Memory Against Istelf in Germany Today," *Critical Inquiry*, 18, Winter 1992, pp. 267–296.

40 Cited in Young, "Jochen Gerz's Countermonuments," p. 120.

41 Roberto Fernández Droguett, "Memoria y conmemoración del golpe de estado de 1973 en Chile: La marcha del 11 de septiembre desde una perspectiva auto-etnográfica," Master's thesis, Universidad Arcis, April 2006, p. 77; Marcia Andrea Escobar, "Cuerpo y memoria: el performance como una forma del recuerdo," Master's thesis, Universidad ARCIS, August 2006, p. 6.

42 Escobar, "Cuerpo y memoria," 2006, p. 7.

43 Equipo peruano de antropología forense (EPAF) press release, August 18, 2009. Campaign blog: http://abretuparaguas.blogspot.com (accessed August 19, 2009).

44 Julia Bryan-Wilson, "Building a Marker of Nuclear Warning," in Robert S. Nelson and Margaret Olin, Eds., *Monuments Made and Unmade*, p. 185.

45 Michael Rothberg, *Multidirectional Memory: Remembering the Holocaust in the Age of Decolonization*, Stanford, CA: Stanford University Press, 2009.

46 Marianne Hirsch, "The Generation of Postmemory," *Poetics Today* 29 (1), Spring 2008, p. 124. See also Claire Kahane, "Dark Mirrors: A Feminist Reflection on Holocaust Narrative and the Maternal Metaphor," in Elisabeth Bronfen and Misha Kavka, Eds., *Feminist Consequences: Gender and Culture*, New York: Columbia University Press, 2000, pp. 161–188. Eva Hoffman refers to the postmemory generation as the "guardians" of the Holocaust. See her *After Such Knowledge: Memory, History, and the Legacy of the Holocaust*, New York: Public Affairs, 2004.

47 Hirsch, "The Generation of Postmemory," p. 104.

2 Memorializing Spain's narrative of empire

1 For a thorough account of the lengthy process of exhuming and reburying the Nationalist dead in the *Valley of the Fallen* crypt, as well as many other dimensions of the site, see Fernando Olmeda, *El Valle de los Caídos: Una memoria de España*, Madrid: Ediciones Peninsula, 2009.

2 For a useful explanation of key factors that led to the breaking of the silences, see Omar Encarnación, "Reconciliation after Democratization: Coping with the Past in Spain," *Political Science Quarterly*, 123, 2008, 435–459. For an additional analysis of why the silences lasted so long, in both Spain and Chile, see Paloma

Aguilar and Katherine Hite, "Historical Memory and Authoritarian Legacies in Processes of Regime Change: Spain and Chile," in Hite and Paola Cesarini, Eds., *Authoritarian Legacies and Democracy in Latin America and Southern Europe*, South Bend, IN: University of Notre Dame Press, 2004, pp. 191–231.

3 Boletín Oficial del Estado, www.boe.es/aeboe/consultas/bases_datos/doc.php? id=BOE-A-2007–22296 (accessed January 9, 2011).

4 Political scientist Paloma Aguilar has documented the marked "ambivalence" toward the past Spaniards express in public opinion polls. See her "Presencia y ausencia de la guerra civil y del franquismo en la democracia española. Reflexiones en torno a la articulación y ruptura del 'pacto de silencio'," in Julio Aróstegui and François Godicheau, *Memoria y nueva Historiografía de la Guerra Civil*, Marcial Pons, Madrid: en prensa, 2005. See also her *Memory and Amnesia: The Role of the Spanish Civil War in the Transition to Democracy*, New York: Berghahn Books, 2002.

5 Carlos E. Cué and Rafael Fraguas, "Qué hacer con el panteón del franquismo," *El País*, April 3, 2005, p. 7.

6 "El Valle de los Caídos, cerrado y sin fecha de reapertura al politico," *Minutodigital.com*, February 8, 2010, www.minutodigital.com/noticias/2010/02/ 08/el-valle-de-los-caidos-cerrado-y-sin-fecha-de-reapertura-al-publico/ (accessed January 12, 2011).

7 Natalia Junquera, "Máxima tension en el Valle de los Caídos entre neonazis y defesnores de la Memoria Histórica," *El País.com*, November 20, 2010, www. elpais.com/articulo/espana/Maxima/tension/Valle/Caidos/neonazis/defensores/ Memoria/Historica/elpepunac/20101120elpepunac_2/Tes (accessed January 12, 2011).

8 Natalia Junquera, "El Valle de los Caídos abrirá de nuevo el próximo día 19," *El País.com*, December 12, 2010, www.elpais.com/articulo/espana/Valle/Caidos/ abrira/nuevo/proximo/dia/elpepiesp/20101210elpepinac_16/Tes (accessed January 12, 2011).

9 Daniel Sueiro, *La verdadera historia del Valle de los Caídos*, Madrid: SEDMAY Ediciones, 1977, p. 15.

10 Peter C. Kent, "The Vatican and the Spanish Civil War," *European History Quarterly*, 16 (4), October 1986, pp. 441–464.

11 *Boletín Oficial del Estado*, número 226, September 5, 1957.

12 *Boletín Oficial del Estado*, número 111, May 10, 1967.

13 Diego Mendes's account is recounted in Sueiro, *La verdadora historia* pp. 138–140. Juan de Avalos recounted his version in an interview with Katherine Halper, *La memoria es vaga/Memory is Lazy*, 2005, www.katiehalper.com. (accessed September 25, 2011).

14 José Luis Sancho, *Guide to the Santa Cruz del Valle de los Caídos*, Madrid: Patrimonio Nacional, 2003, p. 27.

15 Sueiro, pp. 138–40.

16 Don Justo Pérez de Urbel, *El monumento de Santa Cruz del Valle de los Caídos*, Madrid: Instituto de Estudios Madrileños, 1959, p. 26. Cited in Katherine Halper, "Voices from the *Valley*: *El Valle de los Caídos* in History and Memory," senior thesis, Wesleyan University, 2003.

17 For a detailed, pathbreaking study of the Army of Africa and the Spanish Civil War, see Sebastian Balfour, *Deadly Embrace: Morocco and the Road to the Spanish Civil War*, Oxford: Oxford University Press, 2002. I thank Eva Woods for this reference.

18 Ibid., p. 70.

19 Ibid., pp. 250–253.

20 Ibid., p. 312.
21 Ibid., p. 282.
22 Pérez de Urbel, *El monumento de Santa Cruz*, 1959, p. 29. Cited in Halper, p. 69.
23 Sueiro, *La verdadera historia* pp. 257–260.
24 Fernando Olmeda, *El Valle de los Caídos: Una memoria de España*, Madrid: Ediciones Peninsula, 2009, p. 365.
25 Stanley Payne, *The Franco Regime: 1936–1975*, Madison, WI: University of Wisconsin, 1987, pp. 216–219.
26 "Franco's Foes Get Spain's War Bill," *New York Times* April 2, 1939, p. 34.
27 Payne, *The Franco Regime* citing the Anuario Estadístico de España, 1944–1950, p. 223.
28 Virginia Ródenas, "Valle caído en la desmemoria," *ABC*, Sunday, December 4, 2005, pp. 65–66.
29 Carlos E. Cué/Rafael Fraguas, "Qué hacer con el panteón del franquismo," *El País*, April 3, 2005, p. 7.
30 Paloma Aguilar, "Qué hacer con el Valle de los Caídos? Una reconversión inevitable," *El País*, May 8, 2005, p. 17.
31 Nicolás, Sánchez-Albornoz, "Cuelgamuros: presos políticos para un mausoleo," 2003, Mexico, D.F., Mexico: CEMOS.
32 Carlos E. Cué, "Fuimos nosotros: Francisco Sánchez Ruano pasó 11 años en la cárcel por una bomba en el Valle de los Caídos que no puso. Ayer conoció en París a los autores del atentado," *El País*, November 5, 2004, p. 1.
33 Cited in Katherine Halper, "Voices from the *Valley*: El Valle de los Caidos in History and Memory," senior thesis, Wesleyan University, 2003. p. 112.
34 "Una pequeña bomba casera destruye un puente del Valle de los Caídos," *El País*, May 29, 2005, p. 8.
35 For an elaboration of the state versus citizen conceptualization or monuments, see also Jenny Edkins, *Trauma and the Memory of Politics*, Cambridge: Cambridge University Press, 2003.
36 Jacques Derrida, *Specters of Marx: The State of the Debt, the Work of Mourning, and the New International*, New York: Routledge, 1994.
37 See "Demonstrators blame Madrid bombs on PM's support of US war on Iraq," *Agence France Presse–English*, March 13, 2004; Neil Mackay, Marion Mckeone, and James Cusick, "Spanish police arrest five Muslims as crowds accuse Aznar of cover-up," *The Sunday Herald*, March 14, 2004, p. 1; and Geoff Pingree and Lisa Abend, "After attack, Spaniards channel anger at the polls," *Christian Science Monitor*, March 15, 2004, p. 10.
38 Encarnación, "Reconciliation after Democratization," pp. 435–459.
39 See, for example, Mirta Núñez Díaz-Balart, *Los años del terror: La estrategia de dominio y represión del general Franco*, Madrid: La esfera de los Libros, S.L., 2004; Emilio Silva, Asunción Esteban, Javier Castán, and Pancho Salvador, *La memoria de los olvidados: Un debate sobre el silencio de la represión franquista*, Madrid: Ambito Ediciones, 2004; Emilio Silva and Santiago Macías, *Las fosas de Franco: Los republicanos que el dictador dejó en las cunetas*, Madrid: Editorial Temas de Hoy, 2003; and Julián Casanova, Francisco Espinosa, Consita Mir, and Francisco Moreno Gómez, *Morir, Matar, Sobrevivir: La violencia en la dictadura de Franco*, Barcelona: Crítica, 2002.
40 *El País*, September 22, 2004, p. 26.
41 Gustavo de Aristegui, "Euroworried; It's Folly to Think They Struck Us Simply for Iraq," *The Washington Post*, March 21, 2004, p. B.01.
42 Keith B. Richburg, "Plot Leader in Madrid Sought Help of Al Qaeda; Spain Says Suspect Met with Operative," *The Washington Post*, April 12, 2004, p. A.01.

43 For an important discussion of mappings, as well as some useful world historical maps, see Walter D. Mignolo, *Local Histories/Global Designs: Coloniality, Subaltern Knowledges, and Border Thinking*, Princeton, NJ: Princeton University Press, 2000.
44 Américo Castro, *The Structure of Spanish History*, trans. Edmund L. King, Princeton, NJ: Princeton University Press, 1954, p. 96. Originally published as *España en su historia*, 1948. See also Ronald Surtz, Jamie Ferrán, and Daniel Testa, Eds., *Américo Castro: The Impact of His Thought: Essays to Mark the Centenary of His Birth*, Madison, WI: University of Wisconsin Press, 1988.
45 Lizette Alvarez and Elaine Sciolino, "Deep Unease Over the Future Gnaws at Moroccans in Spain," *New York Times*, March 15, 2004, p. A13.
46 An irruption occurred in 2002, when a small group of Moroccan soldiers erected a Moroccan flag on the tiny Isle of Perejil, considered by Spain to be a part of the Ceuta and Melilla enclaves, approximately 600 feet from the Moroccan mainland. This barren rock, home to goats and wild parsley, became the site of a confrontation between this small band of Moroccan soldiers and a massive Spanish fleet summoned to respond to the erection of the flag. The confrontation between Morocco and Spain over the islet brought US Secretary of State Colin Powell in to oversee a resolution. In informal polls, the vast majority of Spaniards supported Aznar's sending in the fleet. The vast majority of Moroccans seek the return of the enclaves.
47 Fortress Europe was originally a term used during World War II both by the British, on the one hand, and the Nazi regime, on the other, to connote the separation between Nazi-occupied continental Europe and the United Kingdom. Today the term is a negative one that refers to the European Union's extensive system of border patrols and detention camps to stem illegal immigration. This includes the role played by Ceuta and Melilla.
48 See, for example, Goytisolo's translated novel, *State of Siege*, San Fransico, CA: City Lights Books, 2002; as well as his essay collection, *Crónicas sarrracinas*, Madrid: Ruedo Ibérico, and his opinion editorials, "Los mitos fundadores de la nación," *El País*, September 14, 1996, p. 11, and "Todos podemos ser bosnios," *El País*, August 25, 1992, p. 7.
49 Alvarez and Sciolino, "Deep unease over the future," p. A13.
50 Geoff Pingree and Lisa Abend, "Spanish Muslims Decry Al Qaeda," *Christian Science Monitor*, March 14, 2005, p. 6.
51 "Madrid Bombers Get Long Sentences," *BBC News.com*, http://newsvote.bbc.co.uk/mpapps/pagetools/print/news.bbc.co.uk/2/hi/europe/7070827.stm (accessed April 12, 2009).
52 Javier Fesser, *Tres días en el Valle: Mi experiencia benedictina*, Madrid: Ediciones Temas de Hoy, 2005.
53 Number 1, Article 16, Valle de los Caídos, Ley de memoria histórica, 52/2007, http://leymemoria.mjusticia.es/paginas/es/ley_memoria.html (accessed February 25, 2011).
54 Cited in Natalia Junquera, "Todos los partidos, salvo el PP, instan al Gobierno a cumplir la ley de memoria en el Valle de los Caídos," *El País.com*. September 22, 2010, www.elpais.com/articulo/espana/Todos/partidos/salvo/PP/instan/Gobierno/cumplir/ley/memoria/Valle/Caidos/elpepiesp/20100922elpepunac_20/Tes (accessed January 12, 2011).

3 Victims, victimizers, and the question of empathy:
   The Eye that Cries

1 Corte Interamericana de Derechos Humanos, Caso del Penal Miguel Castro Castro vs. Perú, Sentencia de 25 de Noviembre, 2006, www.corteidh.or.cr (accessed October 13, 2011).

2 Ibid., p. 149.

3 Ironically, the idea for the Court's sentencing regarding adding the names to *The Eye that Cries* memorial came from the Peruvian government itself. Back in June 2006, when the Peruvian state presented its version of Castro Castro before the Inter-American Court, the government acknowledged "partial responsibility" for human rights violations. (Transcript, Corte Interamericana de Derechos Humanos, Caso del Penal Miguel Castro Castro vx. Perú, Sentencia de 25 de noviembre de 2006, p. 19. Recently the government official representing Peru before the Court, Oscar Manuel Ayzanoa Vigil, was dismissed, owing allegedly to this controversy.) Nevertheless, according to testimony submitted to the Inter-American Court by the Peruvian government, Peru opposed "the symbolic measure of placing a commemorative plaque in the Castro Castro prison, due to the fact that *there already exists a monument to remember all the victims of the armed conflict* and given that the [Castro Castro] prison is a center that currently functions with the presence of organized detainees [who are] militants of the Communist Party of Peru–Shining Path, and a measure of this type would not be favorable to the prison's internal security nor to measures aimed at Peruvian reconciliation."(Transcript, emphasis added.) Apparently, then, in order *not* to rock the boat, the Inter-American Court heeded Peru's concerns regarding symbolic reparations. Negotiating between state and inter-state bodies over symbolic expressions of the violence produced an unanticipated outcome, an unraveling.

4 "Piden a PCM retiro inmediato de nombre de terroristas en mmonumento 'El ojo que llora'," CPN Radio, January 16, 2007, available through "NotiAprodeh," carlosq@aprodeh.org.pe (accessed June 7, 2007).

5 Mario Vargas Llosa, "El ojo que llora," *El País.com*, January 14, 2007.

6 Mario Vargas Llosa, "El ojo que llora," *El País.com*, January 14, 2007.

7 "Entrevista Lika Mutal: No es un homenaje a los terroristas," *La República*, January 18, 2007.

8 "Marchan en defensa de El ojo que llora," *La Primera*, January 22, 2007, available through "InfoAprodeh," carlosq@up.edu.pe (accessed June 7, 2007).

9 Ibid.

10 For a comprehensive study of the Peruvian human rights movement, see Coletta Youngers, *Violencia política y sociedad civil en el Perú: Historia de la Coordinadora Nacional de Derechos Humanos*, Lima: Instituto de Estudios Peruanos, 2003.

11 See the case study by Renzo Salvador Aroni Sulca, "'Aprendimos a convivir con los senderistas y militares': violencia política y respuesta campesina en Huamanquiquia, 1980–1993," *Investigaciones Sociales* X (17), 2006, pp. 259–283.

12 Degregori, Carlos, Ed., *Las rondas campesinas y la derrota de Sendero Luminoso*, Lima: IEP, 1996. See also the Comisión de la Verdad y Reconciliación, Vol. II, Chapter 1.5, section 2, pp. 439–452, www.cverdad.org.pe/ifinal/zip/TOMO%20 II/CAPITULO%201%20-%20Los%20actores%20armados%20del%20conflicto/ 1.5.%20LOS%20COMITES%20DE%20AUTODEFENSA.zip (accessed on June 6, 2007).

13 Ponciano del Pino and Kimberley Theidon, "'Así es como vive gente': procesos deslocalizados y culturas emergentes," in Carlos Iván Degregori and Gonzalo Portocarrero, Eds., *Cultura y globalización*, Lima: Red para el desarrollo de las ciencias sociales en el Perú, 1999.

14 Kimberly Theidon, "Justice in Transition: The Micropolitics of Reconciliation in Postwar Peru," *Journal of Conflict Resolution*, 50, 2006, p. 436. Here Theidon provides a fascinating account and analysis of the ways villagers do work out the re-entry of ex-combatants into their communities.

15 Theidon, *Entre prójmos: el conflicto armado interno y la política de la reconciliación en el Perú*, Lima: IEP, 2004, pp. 196–217.
16 Ibid.
17 Coletta Youngers, "La promoción de los derechos humanos: las ongs y el estado en el Perú," in John Crabtree, Ed., *Construir instituciones: democracia, desarrollo, y desigualdad en el Perú desde 1980*, Lima: Fondo Editorial de la Pontificia Universidad Católica del Perú, Universidad del Pacífico, y el Instituto de Estudios Peruanos, 2006, pp. 163–188.
18 *Comisión de la Verdad y Reconciliación* Volume IV, Chapter One, Section 3, pp. 11–26, www.cverdad.org.pe/ifinal/zip/TOMO%20IV/SECCION%20TERCERA-Los%20Escenarios%20de%20la%20Violencia/Historias%20Regionales/1.0.INTRODUCCION.zip (accessed on June 6, 2007).
19 Cathy Caruth, "Trauma and Experience: Introduction," in Caruth, Ed., *Trauma: Explorations in Memory*, Baltimore, MD: Johns Hopkins University Press, 1998.
20 See Marita Sturken, "The Remembering of Forgetting: Recovered Memory and the Question of Experience," *Social Text*, 57 (Winter), 1998, pp. 103–125; for a more elaborated exploration of the concept of integration, see Judith Herman, *Trauma and Recovery*, New York: Basic, 1992, pp. 1–47.
21 "No es un homenaje a lost terroristas," *La República*, January 18, 2007, available through "InfroAprodeh," carlosq@up.edu.pe.
22 "Memorial 'El Ojo que Llora'," APRODEH, www.aprodeh.org.pe (accessed January 26, 2007.)
23 Lika Mutal, "Las piedras que lloran," *Caretas*, January 25, 2007, p. 41. In our interview, Mutal also referenced the Reverend Lauren Artiss' writings on labyrinths and spirituality, including *Walking a Sacred Path*.
24 Ibid.
25 "Conversación con Lika Mutal" www.agenciaperu.com/cultural/portada/cvr3/mutal.html (accessed February 14, 2007).
26 Author's interview with Lika Mutal, Lima, Peru, April 27, 2007.
27 Ibid.
28 "Conversación con Lika Mutal," www.agenciaperu.com/cultural/portada/cvr3/mutal.html (accessed February 14, 2007).
29 Author's interview with Doris Caqui, Lima, Peru, April 27, 2007.
30 Author's interview with Mr. Roca, Lima, Peru, April 27, 2007.
31 See Jenny Edkins, "Concentration camp memorials and museums: Dachau and the US Holocaust Memorial Museum," in *Trauma and the Memory of Politics*, Cambridge, UK: Cambridge University Press, 2003, pp. 111–174.
32 Jill Bennett, *Empathic Vision: Affect, Trauma, and Contemporary Art*, Stanford, CA: Stanford University Press, 2005.
33 Author's interview with Lika Mutal, April 27, 2007.
34 Ibid.
35 For a discussion of "literal memory," see Elizabeth Jelin, *Los trabajos de la memoria*, Buenos Aires, Argentina: Siglo XXI, 2002, p. 59. This book has been translated: *State Repression and the Labors of Memory*, Minneapolis, MN: University of Minnesota Press, 2003. See also Tzvetan Todorov, *Les abus de la mémoire*, París: Arléa, 1998.
36 Hal Foster, *The Return of the Real*, as cited in Bennett, *Empathetic Vision*, p. 5. See also Elaine Scarry, *The Body in Pain: The Making and Unmaking of the World*, New York: Oxford University Press, 1985.
37 Bennett, *Empathetic Vision*, p. 10.
38 Ibid., p. 8.
39 Ibid., p. 9.

40 Author's interview with Lika Mutal, April 27, 2007.

41 Personal interview at Casa de la Memoria, Ayacucho, Peru, July 3, 2007.

42 Oscar Valderrama López, "Alan García: 'Al acusar a FFAA se cae en juego del senderismo'," *La Razón*, July 15, 2005. Posted on Asociación Pro-Derechos Humanos (APRODEH) website www/aprodeh.org.pe/servicio/c_infoaprodeh.htm (accessed July 15, 2005).

43 Ibid.

44 www.24horaslibre.com/politica/1190735880.php (accessed November 3, 2010).

45 Personal email correspondence with Lika Mutal, September 27, 2007.

46 For an important analysis of the many tension-ridden interpretations of the violences represented by the reactions to the memorial, see Paulo Drinot, "For whom the eye cries: memory, monumentality, and the ontologies of violence in peru," *Journal of Latin American Cultural Studies*, 18 (1), March 2009, pp. 15–32.

47 Cynthia Milton, "Defacing memory: (un)tying Peru's memory knots," *Memory Studies*, forthcoming.

48 Author's interview with Rosario Narváez, Lima, Peru, April 30, 2007.

49 Ibid.

50 For a moving description of the origin of the idea for the chalina, see www.larepublica.pe/sociedad/25/06/2010/la-chalina-de-la-esperanza (accessed October 26, 2010).

51 Author's interview with Mutal, April 27, 2007.

52 See www.paraquenoserepita.org.pe/regiones/apurimac2.php (accessed October 28, 2010).

53 Personal email correspondence with Lika Mutal, September 26, 2007.

4 Searching and the inter-generational transmission of grief in Paine, Chile

1 The Medical Legal Service claimed fourteen Paine members' remains had been exhumed from an anonymous mass grave in Chile's General Cemetery. This proved to be false.

2 Javier Rebolledo, "El coronel confiesa," *La Nación*, October 15, 2006, accessed at www.lanacion.cl on July 25, 2010.

3 As reported in "Paradero de personas desaparecidas según Informe del Gobierno," *El Mercurio*, January 9, 2001, accessed at www.emol.cl on July 26, 2010.

4 "Human Rights Trials in Chile and the Region Bulletin #7," Human Rights Observatory, Universidad Diego Portales, Santiago, Chile, June 2010.

5 *Report of the Chilean National Commission on Truth and Reconciliation*, translated by Phillip E. Berryman, Volume 1, South Bend, IN: University of Notre Dame Press, p. 246.

6 Karl Mannheim, "The Problem of Generations," in Paul Kecskemeti, Ed., *Essays on the Sociology of Knowledge*, New York: Oxford University Press, 1928, p. 306.

7 See Marianne Hirsch, "Projected Memory: Holocaust Photographs in Personal and Public Fantasy," in Mieke Bal, Jonathan Crewe, and Leo Spitzer, Eds., *Acts of Memory: Cultural Recall in the Present*, Hanover, NH: University Press of New England, 1999, pp. 3–23.

8 For the classic text on Chile's political party system and the elements that led to Chile's democratic demise, see Arturo Valenzuela, *The Breakdown of Democratic Regimes: Chile*, Baltimore, MD: Johns Hopkins University Press, 1979.

9 For a discussion of the effects of Chilean state and ruling class concentration on mining and industrial production at the expense of agricultural production in the 1940s and 1950s, see Fernando Henrique Cardoso and Enzo Faletto, *Dependency*

and Development in Latin America, Berkeley, CA: University of California Press,
   1979 (Marjory Mattingly Urquidi translator); Brian Loveman, *Chile: The Legacy
   of Hispanic Capitalism*, New York: Oxford University Press, 1988.
10 Loveman, *Chile*.
11 Jacques Chonchol, *Sistemas agrarios en América Latina: de la etapa prehispánica;
   a modernización conservadora*. Cited in Juan René Maureira Moreno, "Enfrentar
   con la vida a la muerte: Historia y memorias de la violencia y el Terrorismo de
   Estado en Paine (1960–2008)," Thesis for a Licenciado en Historia, University of
   Chile, January 2009.
12 For more detailed analysis of the 1960s Chilean left leadership, see Katherine Hite,
   When the Romance Ended: Leaders of the Chilean Left, 1968–1998, New York:
   Columbia University Press, 2000.
13 See Peter Kornbluh, *Pinochet File: A Declassified Dossier on Atrocity and
   Accountability*, New York: The New Press, 2004.
14 J.R. Maureira, "Enfrentar con la vida a la muerte."
15 In addition to Juan René Maureira's thesis, I benefited enormously for this chapter
   from the detailed study and analysis of four centuries of the history of Rangue,
   by Nicolás Ocaranza, "Rangue: Del latifundio al Chile postdictatorial," in Andrés
   Baeza, Andrés Estefane, Juan Luis Ossa, Joaquín Fernández, Cristóbal García-
   Huidobro, Nicolás Ocaranza, and Pablo Moscoso, *XX: Historias del siglo veinte*,
   Santiago, Chile: Grupo Zeta, 2008, pp. 303–391.
16 Interview with Gabriela Ortíz, Santiago, Chile, July 9, 2009.
17 Ocaranza, "Rangue," pp. 318–320.
18 Interview with Juan René Maureira, Santiago, Chile, January 5, 2009. For an
   additional, detailed account of Sonia Carreño's testimony and others, see Patricia
   Verdugo, *Tiempo de días claros: los desaparecidos*, Santiago, Chile: CESOC, 1990,
   pp. 13–38.
19 Ocaranza, "Rangue," pp. 369–370.
20 Ibid., p. 363.
21 Ibid., p. 378.
22 Ruby Weitzel, *El callejón de las viudas*, Santiago: Editorial Planeta, 2001, pp.
   203–205. Weitzel provides a detailed journalistic account of the ordeal of many
   of Paine's widows.
23 Ocaranza, "Rangue," pp. 393.
24 On October 16, 2010, exactly thirty-seven years after René Maureira's abduction,
   Maureira's wife Sonia Carreño and the Medical Legal Service confirmed that among
   the remains of the exhumed at Aculeo were the glasses and a piece of the pant
   leg of René Maureira. See CNN-Chile report: www.cnnchile.com/nacional/2010/
   10/16/sml-entrego-restos-oseos-de-victimas-del-caso-paine/ (accessed October 18,
   2010).
25 Jorge Escalante, "La confesión del teniente Andrés Magaña," *La Nacion*,
   September 27, 2007, accessed at www.lanacion.cl on July 25, 2010.
26 Dori Laub, "Truth and Testimony: The Process and the Struggle," in Cathy
   Caruth, Ed., *Trauma: Explorations in Memory*, Baltimore, MD: Johns Hopkins
   University Press, 1998, p. 61.
27 Weitzel, *El callejón de las viudas*, pp. 110–117.
28 Laub, "Truth and Testimony," p. 66.
29 Weitzel, *El callejón de las viudas*, pp. 117–126.
30 Some Paine families, like the family of René Maureira, do not have a death
   certificate. Sonia Carreño maintains her civil status as "married," not "widowed."
31 C.S. Lewis, *A Grief Observed*, San Francisco: Harper Collins, 1961, p. 15.
32 Ibid.

33 To view a typical description of the seven stages of grief, visit: www.recover-from-grief.com/7-stages-of-grief.html (accessed September 23, 2010).

34 Didion, *The Year of Magical Thinking*, p. 169. I thank Lisa Gail Collins for reading and thinking about Didion with me.

35 Ibid., pp. 188–195.

36 J.R. Maureira, "Enfrentar la vida a la muerte," pp. 96–97.

37 Weitzel, *El callejón de las viudas*, pp. 163–168.

38 J.R. Maureira, "Enfrentar la vida a la muerte," pp. 97–98.

39 Ibid., p. 98.

40 Weitzel, *El callejón de las viudas*, pp. 122–128.

41 J.R. Maureira, "Enfrentar con la vida a la muerte," pp. 98–99.

42 Hirsch, "The Generation of Post-memory," *Poetics Today* 29(1), Spring 2008, pp. 103–128.

43 Ibid.

44 Alejandra Oberti, "La flexion del sí mismo en las interpretaciones de la violencia política," Segundo Congreso Internacional Comunicación y Política, Universidad Metropolitana Xochimilco, México, November 2005, www.elortiba.org/oberti.html (accessed September 27, 2010).

45 Jacques Hassoun, *Los contrabandistas de la memoria*, Buenos Aires: Ediciones de la Flor, 1996, cited in Oberti.

46 Oberti, "La flexion," (pages not numbered).

47 Hirsch, "The Generation of Post-memory," p. 115.

48 Gustavo Germano, *Ausencias*, Barcelona: Casa América Catalunya, 2007. See also www.gustavogermano.com/ (accessed September 29, 2010).

49 For a close, nuanced analysis of this effect, see Rubén Chababo, "Clara Atelman de Fink," posted at http://ausencias-gustavogermano.blogspot.com/ (accessed September 28, 2010).

50 Patricio Guzmán, *Nostalgia por la luz*, www.youtube.com/watch?v=yEuKPdlC6gs (accessed September 27, 2010).

51 Ibid.

52 See also Isabel Piper, "Obstinaciones de la memoria: la dictadura military chilena en las tramas del recuerdo," Doctoral Thesis in Social Psychology, Autonomous University of Barcelona, Spain, 2005.

53 *Declaración de objetivos de la Agrupación de Familiares de Detenidos Desaparecidos de Paine*, 2000. Included in J.R. Maureira, "Enfrentar con la vida a la muerte," pp. 107–108.

54 For a detailed analysis of the Allende monument, see Katherine Hite, "El monumento a Allende y la política chilena," in Elizabeth Jelin and Victoria Langland, Eds., *Monumentos, memoriales y marcas territoriales* Volume 5, Mexico: Siglo XXI, 2003, pp. 19–56. For a nuanced discussion of Morandé 80 and other commemorative symbols and dates, see Alfredo Joignant, *Un día distinto: Memorias festivas y batallas conmemorativas en torno al 11 de septiembre en Chile 1974–2006*, Santiago: Editorial Universitaria, 2007.

55 http://afddpaine.blogspot.com/2006/03/en-definitiva-la-cultura-de-la-vida.html (accessed January 15, 2010).

56 Author's visit to Paine and meeting with the Association, January 7, 2009. Some thirty-five members attended the Association's monthly meeting.

57 Interview with Juan René Maureira, Santiago, January 5, 2009.

58 Interview with Gabi Ortiz, December 11, 2010.

59 Fernando Coronil, "Seeing History," *Hispanic American Historical Review*, 84 (1), 2004, p. 2.

60 Elizabeth Jelin and Victorial Langland, "Introducción. Las marcas territoriales como nexo entre pasado presente," in Jelin and Langland, Eds., *Monumentos, memoriales y marcas territoriales*, Buenos Aires and Madrid: Siglo XXI, 2003, p. 2.
61 Interview with Juan René Maureira, January 5, 2009.

5 The globality of art and memory making: The *bicis* of Fernando Traverso

1 *Los Desaparecidos* (The Disappeared) was an exhibit of the works of fourteen Latin American artists, as well as a piece by one artists' collective. Curated by Laurel Reuter of the North Dakota Museum of Art, the show opened in Grand Forks, North Dakota, and then traveled to Buenos Aires and Montevideo before it came to El Museo del Barrio in New York City in 2007. The exhibit traveled next to Lima, and then to Santa Fe, New Mexico, Santiago, Chile, Bogotá, Colombia, the Organization of American States in Washington, DC, Laramie, Wyoming, and finally to Minneapolis, Minnesota.
2 For a fascinating analysis of these monuments and others, see Kirk Savage, "The Politics of Memory: Black Emancipation and the Civil War Monument," in John R. Gillis, Ed., *Commemorations: The Politics of National Identity*, Princeton, NJ: Princeton University Press, 1994, pp. 127–149.
3 In Diego Fidulgo, *Trescientoscincuenta*, a documentary on Traverso's work (accessed May 10, 2011).
4 Interview with Fernando Traverso, Rosario, Argentina, July 26, 2008.
5 The ongoing story of the Ché monument in Rosario is interwoven with class and revolutionary politics in and of itself. To come up with the approximately three tons of quite expensive metal bronze to sculpt the twelve-foot-high statue, the artist entreated Rosarinos and other Argentines around the world to donate bronze keys. According to the website, 14,454 people participated, donating 75,000 keys. The monument can thus be described as a "collective work." In 2009, the monument was attacked, and apparently the attackers intended to cut the figure's legs off, though they were unsuccessful. See: http://monumentoalcherosario.wordpress.com/ (accessed November 14, 2010).
6 See James E. Young, *The Texture of Memory: Holocaust Memorials and Meaning*, New Haven, CT: Yale University Press, 1993, pp. 43–47.
7 Rubén Chababo, presenter, "En torno al Museo de la Memoria (Rosario, Argentina)," *Uso público de los sitios históricos para la transmisión de la memoria*, Buenos Aires: Memoria Abierta, June 8–10, 2006, p. 9.
8 To date, thanks to the persistence of the Grandmothers of the Plaza de Mayo and DNA technology, 101 Argentine citizens have been positively identified as children who were either born in captivity or kidnapped in very early childhood by Argentine security forces during the dictatorship.
9 Personal communication with the author, July 23, 2010.
10 Personal communication with the author, July 25, 2008.
11 Traverso's interview with Rubén Chababo, *Diario La Capital de Rosario*, January 4, 2004, available: www.00350.com.ar, November 15, 2010.
12 "Eduardo Favario: Entre la pintura y la acción," in the exhibit brochure, *Tinta Roja: Represión a la cultura durante la última dictadura militar 1976–1983*, Rosario: Museo de la Memoria, March 2004. Favario's work was a centerpiece of this exhibit, and it was the first time in a show of the artist's work that the ERP insignia was also publicly displayed.
13 Carlos Nino, *Radical Evil on Trial*, New Haven, CT: Yale University Press, 1996, p. 104.

14 Marguerite Feitlowitz, *A Lexicon of Terror: Argentina and the Legacies of Torture*, New York: Oxford University Press, 1998.
15 The term "insile" represents a significant number of Argentines, including Fernando Traverso, who went into hiding or were forced to begin new lives in other parts of the country. When he was in exile in Corrientes, Traverso survived with a friend, selling little souvenir flags of Antonio Gil, a popular saint-like gaucho of northern Argentina.
16 Susana Kaiser, *Postmemories of Terror: A New Generation Copes with the Legacy of the "Dirty War,"* New York: Palgrave Macmillan, 2005.
17 María Sondereguer, "El debate sobre el pasado reciente en Argentina," *Punto de Vista* XXIX, no. 87, December 2000, pp. 3–15.
18 Vincent Druliolle, "Silhouettes of the Disappeared: Memory, Justice and Human Rights in Post-Authoritarian Argentina," *Human Rights and Human Welfare*, no. 9, 2009, p. 80. Druliolle offers a very thoughtful review of the *Silhuetazo*, placing the silhouettes and the disappeared themselves in historical context. He writes, "At the turn of the twenty-first century, the disappeared had returned to Argentine society, no longer as invisible traces haunting daily life, but as acknowledged absences," p. 77.
19 Sondereguer, "El debate sobre el pasado reciente en Argentina."
20 Sondereguer, "El debate sobre el pasado reciente en Argentina," pp. 6–9.
21 Ana Longoni, "Traiciones. La figura del traidor (y la traidora) en los relatos acerca de los sobrevivientes de la repression," in Elizabeth Jelin and Ana Longoni, Eds., *Escrituras, imágenes y escenarios ante la repression*, Buenos Aires: Siglo XXI, 2005, p. 215.
22 As paraphrased by Antjie Krog in her *Country of My Skull: Guilt, Sorrow, and the Limits of Forgiveness in the New South Africa*, New York: Three Rivers Press, 2000, p. 147.
23 See www.leonferrari.com.ar/index.php?/bio/ (accessed November 14, 2010). For a montage of his clippings, entitled, "Nosotros no sabíamos." See www.leon ferrari.com.ar/index.php?/series/nosotros-no-sabiamos/(accessed December 5, 2010). See also "La fragata Libertad," reproduced in Marcelo Brodksy, *Memoria en construcción: el debate sobre la ESMA*, Buenos Aires: la marca editora, 2005, p. 121.
24 "Por su cercanía física, por estar en medio de la sociedad, *del otro lado de la pared*, el campo de concentración sólo puede existir en medio de una sociedad que elige no ver."
25 Rubén Chababo, "Our Face in the Mirror: Military Dictatorship and Civil Society," Vassar College, November 11, 2008.
26 Oliver Galak, "Controversia por el prólogo agregado al informe "'Nunca más'." Translated by author. *La Nación*, May 19, 2006, www.lanacion.com.ar/nota.asp? nota_id=807208 (accessed April 17, 2010).
27 Patricia Tappatá de Valdez, "El Parque de la Memoria en Buenos Aires," in Elizabeth Jelin and Victoria Langland, Eds., *Monumentos, memoriales, y marcas territoriales*, Buenos Aires and Madrid: Siglo XXI, pp. 97–110.
28 See photograph of *El pañol* installation, 1999, *Memoria en construcción: el debate sobre la ESMA*, Buenos Aires: la marca editora, 2005, p. 139.
29 Brodsky, *Memoria en construcción*, p. 219.
30 Andreas Huyssen, "El arte mnemónico de Marcelo Brodsky/The Mnemonic Art of Marcelo Brodsky," in Marcelo Brodsky, *Nexo: un ensayo fotográfico/ A photographic essay*, Buenos Aires: Centro Cultural Recoleta, 2001, p. 9.
31 For descriptions and the intents of the sculptures, see the catalogue produced by the Comisión Pro Monumento a las Vícitmas del Terrorismo del Estado, "Proyecto

Parque de la memoria," Buenos Aires: Gobierno de Buenos Aires, 2005. The catalogue is in Spanish and English.

32 Traverso's interview with Rubén Chababo, *Diario La Capital de Rosario*, January 4, 2004, available: www.00350.com.ar/ (accessed November 15, 2010).

33 Diario La Capital de Rosario, January 4, 2004, available: www.00350.com.ar/ (accessed November 15, 2010).

34 Grupo En Trámite, http://entramite.wokitoki.com.ar/enlacalle.html (accessed March 23, 2007).

35 Interview with Fernando Traverso, Rosario, Argentina, December 18, 2010.

36 Interview with Marcelo Brodsky, Buenos Aires, April 18, 2007.

37 Alessandro Portelli, *The Death of Luigi Trastulli and Other Stories: Form and Meaning in Oral History*, Albany, NY: SUNY Press, 1991.

38 Michael Rothberg, *Multidirectional Memory: Remembering the Holocaust in the Age of Decolonization*, Stanford, CA: Stanford University Press, 2009.

39 Interview with Fernando Traverso, December 18, 2010.

Epilogue

1 As Juan René also explained to me, in practical terms, it proves impossible completely to separate, to individuate the remains. The final burial remains of the nine men came in seven boxes—four that the Legal Medical Service identified as four individuals, and three that the Service claimed were impossible to separate. Interview, Buenos Aires, December 19, 2010.

2 Interview with Juan Leonardo Maureira, Paine, Chile, December 12, 2010.

3 The statistics come from the Human Rights Observatory of the Universidad Diego Portales, directed by Cath Collins. The Observatory maintains a meticulous database of human rights cases and prosecutions and publishes a bilingual monthly bulletin on human rights issues in Chile and the region: www.icso.cl/observatorio-derechos-humanos/ (accessed October 5, 2010).

4 Interview with Juan René Maureira, Buenos Aires, Argentina, December 19, 2010.

5 Videographers posted a ten-minute video of Traverso's workshop on the radical website Antenamutante.net: www.antenamutante.net/ (accessed December 28, 2010).

6 Interview with Lika Mutal, November 8, 2010.

7 Consejo de Reparaciones Registro Unico de Víctimas, *Reporte: Información sobre víctimas y beneficiarios del Programa de Reparaciones Económicas*, December 31, 2010. www.ruv.gob.pe/ (accessed February 1, 2011).

8 For her important critical interpretation of US engagement with the country's traumatic sites of history and memory, including the 9/11 site, see Sturken, *Tourists of History: Memory, Kitsch, and Consumerism from Oklahoma City to Ground Zero*, Durham, NC: Duke University Press, 2007.

9 Chababo, "Our Face in the Mirror," Vassar College, November 11, 2008.

Bibliography

Press

Aguilar, Paloma, "Qué hacer con el Valle de los Caídos? Una reconversión inevitable," *El País*, May 8, 2005, p. 17.

Alvarez, Lizette and Elaine Sciolino, "Deep Unease Over the Future Gnaws at Moroccans in Spain," *New York Times*, March 15, 2004.

Antenamutante.net: www.antenamutante.net/ (accessed December 28, 2010).

Chababo, Rubén. "Interview with Fernando Traverso," *Diario La Capital de Rosario*, January 4, 2004, available: www.00350.com.ar/ (accessed November 15, 2010).

CNN–Chile report: www.cnnchile.com/nacional/2010/10/16/sml-entrego-restos-oseos-de-victimas-del-caso-paine/ (accessed October 18, 2010).

"Conversación con Lika Mutal," www.agenciaperu.com/cultural/portada/cvr3/mutal.html (accessed February 14, 2007).

Cué, Carlos E., "Fuimos nosotros: Francisco Sánchez Ruano pasó 11 años en la cárcel por una bomba en el Valle de los Caídos que no puso. Ayer conoció en París a los autores del atentado," *El País*, November 5, 2004.

Cué, Carlos E. and Rafael Fraguas, "Qué hacer con el panteón del franquismo," *El País*, April 3, 2005.

De Aristegui, Gustavo, "Euroworried; It's Folly to Think They Struck Us Simply for Iraq," *The Washington Post*, March 21, 2004.

"Demonstrators blame Madrid bombs on PM's support of US war on Iraq," Agence France Presse–English, March 13, 2004.

"Entrevista Lika Mutal: No es un homenaje a los terroristas," *La República*, January 18, 2007.

"Equipo peruano de antropología forense," (EPAF) press release, August 18, 2009.

Escalante, Jorge, "La confesión del teniente Andrés Magaña," *La Nación*, September 27, 2007, www.lanacion.cl (accessed July 25, 2010).

"Franco's Foes Get Spain's War Bill," *New York Times*, April 2, 1939, p. 34.

Galak, Oliver, "Controversia por el prólogo agregado al informe 'Nunca más'." Translated by author. *La Nación*, May 19, 2006, www.lanacion.com.ar/nota.asp?nota_id=807208 (accessed April 17, 2010).

Goytisolo, Juan, "Todos podemos ser bosnios," *El País*, August 25, 1992, p. 7.

Goytisolo, Juan, "Los mitos fundadores de la nación," *El País*, September 14, 1996, p. 11.

Junquera, Natalia, "Todos los partidos, salvo el PP, instan al Gobierno a cumplir la ley de memoria en el Valle de los Caídos," El País.com, September 22, 2010, www.elpais.com/articulo/espana/Todos/partidos/salvo/PP/instan/Gobierno/cumplir/ley/memoria/Valle/Caidos/elpepiesp/20100922elpepunac_20/Tes (accessed January 12, 2011).

Junquera, Natalia, "Máxima tension en el Valle de los Caídos entre neonazis y defensores de la Memoria Histórica," El País.com, November 20, 2010, www.elpais.com/articulo/espana/Maxima/tension/Valle/Caidos/neonazis/defensores/Memoria/Historica/elpepunac/20101120elpepunac_2/Tes (accessed January 12, 2011).

Junquera, Natalia, "El Valle de los Caídos abrirá de nuevo el próximo día 19," El País.com, December 12, 2010, www.elpais.com/articulo/espana/Valle/Caidos/abrira/nuevo/proximo/dia/elpepiesp/20101210elpepinac_16/Tes. (accessed January 12, 2011).

www.larepublica.pe/sociedad/25/06/2010/la-chalina-de-la-esperanza (accessed October 26, 2010).

Mackay, Neil, Marion McKeone and Jane Cusick, "Spanish police arrest five Muslims as crowds accuse Aznar of cover-up," *The Sunday Herald*, March 14, 2004.

"Marchan en defensa de El ojo que llora," *La Primera*, January 22, 2007, available through "InfoAprodeh," carlosq@up.edu.pe (accessed June 7, 2007).

Mutal, Lika, "Las piedras que lloran, " *Caretas*, January 25, 2007, p. 41.

"No es un homenaje a lost terroristas," *La República*, January 18, 2007, available through "InfoAprodeh," carlosq@up.edu.pe (accessed June 7, 2007).

"Paradero de personas desaparecidas según Informe del Gobierno," *El Mercurio*, January 9, 2001, www.emol.cl (accessed July 26, 2010).

"Piden a PCM retiro inmediato de nombre de terroristas en mmonumento 'El ojo que llora'," CPN Radio, January 16, 2007, available through "NotiAprodeh," carlosq@aprodeh.org.pe (accessed June 7, 2007).

Pingree, Geoff and Lisa Abend, "After attack, Spaniards channel anger at the polls," *Christian Science Monitor*, March 15, 2004.

Pingree, Geoff and Lisa Abend, "Spanish Muslims decry Al Qaeda," *Christian Science Monitor*, March 14, 2005.

Rebolledo, Javier, "El coronel confiesa," *La Nación*, October 15, 2006, www.lanacion.cl (accessed July 25, 2010).

Richburg, Keith B., "Plot Leader in Madrid Sought Help of Al Qaeda; Spain Says Suspect Met with Operative," *The Washington Post*, April 12, 2004.

Ródenas, Virginia, "Valle caído en la desmemoria," *ABC*, Sunday, December 4, 2005.

"Una pequeña bomba casera destruye un puente del Valle de los Caídos," *El País*, May 29, 2005, p. 8.

Vargas Llosa, Mario, "El ojo que llora," *El País.com*, January 14, 2007.

Online documentary material and cited organization websites

http://afddpaine.blogspot.com/2006/03/en-definitiva-la-cultura-de-la-vida.html (accessed January 4, 2010).

www.aprodeh.org.pe/aprodeh2009/index.php (accessed June 26, 2007).

Arlington West, www.arlingtonwestsantamonica.org/ (accessed July 18, 2008).

Campaign blog: http://abretuparaguas.blogspot.com (accessed August 19, 2009).

Comisión de la Verdad y Reconciliación, Volume II, Chapter 1.5, section 2, www.cverdad.org.pe/ifinal/zip/TOMO%20II/CAPITULO%201%20-%20Los%20actores%20armados%20del%20conflicto/1.5.%20LOS%20COMITES%20DE%20

AUTODEFENSA.zip (accessed June 6, 2007).

Comisión de la Verdad y Reconciliación, Volume IV, Chapter One, Section 3, www. cverdad.org.pe/ifinal/zip/TOMO%20IV/SECCION%20TERCERA-Los%20Escenarios %20de%20la%20Violencia/Historias%20Regionales/ 1.0.INTRODUCCION.zip (accessed June 6, 2007).

Consejo de Reparaciones Registro Unico de Víctimas, Reporte: Información sobre víctimas y beneficiarios del Programa de Reparaciones Económicas, December 31, 2010, www.ruv.gob.pe/ (accessed February 1, 2011).

Grupo En Trámite, http://entramite.wokitoki.com.ar/enlacalle.html (accessed March 23, 2007).

Fidulgo, Diego, *Trescientoscincuenta*, www.trescientoscincuenta.blogspot.com/ (accessed May 10, 2011).

www.gustavogermano.com/ (accessed September 29, 2010).

Guzmán, Patricio, *Nostalgia por la luz*, www.youtube.com/watch?v=yEuKPdlC6gs (accessed September 27, 2010).

Human Rights Observatory of the Universidad Diego Portales, www.icso.cl/ observatorio-derechos-humanos (accessed October 5, 2010).

"Human Rights Trials in Chile and the Region Bulletin #7," Human Rights Observatory, Universidad Diego Portales, Santiago, Chile, June 2010, www.icso.cl/ observatorio-derechos-humanos/ (accessed October 13, 2011).

www.leonferrari.com.ar/index.php?/series/nosotros-no-sabiamos (accessed December 5, 2010).

http://monumentoalcherosario.wordpress.com/ (accessed November 14, 2010).

www.paraquenoserepita.org.pe/regiones/apurimac2.php (accessed October 28, 2010).

Peace Ribbon Project, www.codepink4peace.org/section.php?id=17 (accessed November 1, 2010).

www.recover-from-grief.com/7-stages-of-grief.html (accessed September 23, 2010).

Valderrama López, Oscar, "Alan García: 'Al acusar a FFAA se cae en juego del senderismo'," *La Razón*, July 15, 2005. Posted on Asociación Pro-Derechos Humanos (APRODEH) website, www/aprodeh.org.pe/servicio/c_infoaprodeh.htm (accessed July 15, 2005).

"El Valle de los Caídos, cerrado y sin fecha de reapertura al politico," Minuto digital.com, February 8, 2010, www.minutodigital.com/noticias/2010/02/08/el-valle-de-los-caidos-cerrado-y-sin-fecha-de-reapertura-al-publico/ (accessed January 12, 2011.

Texts

Aguilar, Paloma, *Memory and Amnesia: The Role of the Spanish Civil War in the Transition to Democracy*, New York: Berghahn Books, 2002.

Aguilar, Paloma, "Presencia y ausencia de la guerra civil y del franquismo en la democracia española. Reflexiones en torno a la articulación y ruptura del 'pacto de silencio'," in Julio Aróstegui and François Godicheau, Eds., *Memoria y nueva Historiografía de la Guerra Civil*, Madrid: Marcial Pons, 2006, pp. 245–293.

Aguilar, Paloma and Katherine Hite, "Historical Memory and Authoritarian Legacies in Processes of Regime Change: Spain and Chile," in Katherine Hite and Paola Cesarini, Eds., *Authoritarian Legacies and Democracy in Latin America and Southern Europe*, South Bend, IN: University of Notre Dame Press, 2004, pp. 191–231.

Anuario Estadístico de España, 1944–1950.

Assmann, Jan, "Collective Memory and Cultural Identity," *New German Critique*, 65, Cultural History/Cultural Studies, Spring–Summer, 1995, pp. 125–133.

Balfour, Sebastian, *Deadly Embrace: Morocco and the Road to the Spanish Civil War*, Oxford: Oxford University Press, 2002.

Bennett, Jill, *Empathic Vision: Affect, Trauma, and Contemporary Art*, Stanford, CA: Stanford University Press, 2005.

Boletín Oficial del Estado (Spain), número 226, September 5, 1957.

Boletín Oficial del Estado (Spain), número 111, May 10, 1967.

Brown, Wendy, *Politics Out of History*, Princeton, NJ: Princeton University Press, 2001.

Butler, Judith, *Precarious Life: The Powers of Mourning and Violence*, London: Verso Books, 2004.

Bryan-Wilson, Julia, "Building a Marker of Nuclear Warning," in Robert S. Nelson and Margaret Olin, Eds., *Monuments Made and Unmade*, Chicago, IL: University of Chicago Press, 2003, pp. 183–203.

Caruth, Cathy, "Trauma and Experience: Introduction," in Caruth, Ed., *Trauma: Explorations in Memory*, Baltimore, MD: Johns Hopkins University Press, 1998.

Casanova, Julián, Francisco Espinosa, Consita Mir, and Francisco Moreno Gómez, *Morir, Matar, Sobrevivir: La violencia en la dictadura de Franco*, Barcelona: Crítica, 2002.

Castro, Américo, *The Structure of Spanish History*, trans. Edmund L. King, Princeton, NJ: Princeton University Press, 1954. Originally published as *España en su historia*, 1948.

Catalogue produced by the Comisión Pro Monumento a las Víctimas del Terrorismo del Estado, *Proyecto Parque de la memoria*, Buenos Aires: Gobierno de Buenos Aires, 2005. The catalogue is in Spanish and English.

Chababo, Rubén, "En torno al Museo de la Memoria (Rosario, Argentina),"*Uso público de los sitios históricos para la transmisión de la memoria*, Buenos Aires: Memoria Abierta, June 8–10, 2006.

Chababo, Rubén, "Our Face in the Mirror: Military Dictatorship and Civil Society," Vassar College, November 11, 2008.

Chonchol, Jacques, *Sistemas agrarios en América Latina: de la etapa prehispánica a la modernización conservadora.* Cited in Juan René Maureira Moreno, "Enfrentar con la vida a la muerte: Historia y memorias de la violencia y el Terrorismo de Estado en Paine (1960–2008)," Thesis for a Licenciado en Historia, University of Chile, January 2009.

Coronil, Fernando, "Seeing History," *Hispanic American Historical Review*, 84 (1), 2000, pp. 139–141.

Corte Interamericana de Derechos Humanos, *Caso del Penal Miguel Castro Castro vs. Perú*, Sentencia de 25 de Noviembre, 2006, www.corteidh.or.cr (accessed October 13, 2011).

Danto, Arthur, "The Vietnam Veterans Memorial," *The Nation*, August 31, 1986, p. 152. Cited in James E. Young, *The Texture of Memory: Holocaust Memorials and Meaning*, New Haven, CT: Yale University Press, 1993.

Degregori, Carlos, Ed., *Las rondas campesinas y la derrota de Sendero Luminoso*, Lima: IEP, 1996.

Declaración de objetivos de la Agrupación de Familiares de Detenidos Desaparecidos de Paine, 2000. Included in Juan René Maureira Moreno, "Enfrentar con la vida a la muerte: Historia y memorias de la violencia y el Terrorismo de Estado en Paine (1960–2008)," January 2009.

Del Pino, Ponciano and Kimberley Theidon, "'Así es como vive gente': procesos deslocalizados y culturas emergentes," in Carlos Iván Degregori and Gonzalo Portocarrero, Eds., *Cultura y globalización*, Lima: Red para el desarrollo de las ciencias sociales en el Perú, 1999.

Derrida, Jacques, *Specters of Marx: The State of the Debt, the Work of Mourning, and the New International*, New York: Routledge, 1994.

Didion, Joan, *The Year of Magical Thinking*, New York: Vintage International edition, 2007.

Drinot, Paulo, "For Whom the Eye Cries: Memory, Monumentality, and the Ontologies of Violence in Peru," *Journal of Latin American Cultural Studies*, 18 (1), March 2009, pp. 15–32.

Druliolle, Vincent, "Silhouettes of the Disappeared: Memory, Justice and Human Rights in Post-Authoritarian Argentina," *Human Rights and Human Welfare*, Volume 9, 2009.

Edkins, Jenny, *Trauma and the Memory of Politics*, Cambridge, UK: Cambridge University Press, 2003.

"Eduardo Favario: Entre la pintura y la acción," in *Tinta Roja: Represión a la cultura durante la última dictadura militar 1976–1983*, Rosario: Museo de la Memoria, March 2004.

Encarnación, Omar, "Reconciliation after Democratization: Coping with the Past in Spain," *Political Science Quarterly*, 123 (3), 2008, pp. 453–459.

Escobar, Maria Andrea, "Cuerpo y memoria: el performance como una forma del recuerdo," Master's thesis, Universidad ARCIS, August 2006.

Feitlowitz, Marguerite, *A Lexicon of Terror: Argentina and the Legacies of Torture*, New York: Oxford University Press, 1998.

Fernández Droguett, Roberto, "Memoria y conmemoración del golpe de estado de 1973 en Chile: La marcha del 11 de septiembre desde una perspectiva autoetnográfica," Master's thesis, Universidad Arcis, April 2006.

Ferretti, Maria, "Nostalgia for Communism in Post-Soviet Russia," unpublished paper.

Fesser, Javier, *Tres días en el Valle: Mi experiencia benedictina*, Madrid: Ediciones Temas de Hoy, 2005.

"La fragata Libertad," reproduced in Marcelo Brodksy, *Memoria en construcción: el debate sobre la ESMA*, Buenos Aires: la marca editora, 2005.

Gell, Alfred, *Art and Agency: An Anthroplogical Theory*, Oxford: Oxford University Press, 1998.

Germano, Gustavo, *Ausencias*, Barcelona, Spain: Casa América Catalunya, 2007.

Goytisolo, Juan, *State of Siege*, San Fransico, CA: City Lights Books, 2002.

Goytisolo, Juan, *Crónicas sarrracinas*, Madrid: Ruedo Ibérico, 1982.

Halper, Katherine, *La memoria es vaga/Memory is Lazy*, documentary, 2005.

Hass, Kristin Ann *Carried to the Wall: American Memory and the Vietnam Veterans Memorial*, Berkeley, CA: University of California Press, 1998.

Hassoun, Jacques, *Los contrabandistas de la memoria*, Buenos Aires: Ediciones de la Flor, 1996.

Herman, Judith, *Trauma and Recovery*, New York: Basic, 1992.

Hirsch, Marianne, "Projected Memory: Holocaust Photographs in Personal and Public Fantasy," in Mieke Bal, Jonathan Crewe, and Leo Spitzer, Eds., *Acts of Memory:*

Cultural Recall in the Present, Hanover, NH: University Press of New England, 1999, pp. 3–23.

Hirsch, Marianne, "The Generation of Postmemory," *Poetics Today*, 29 (1), Spring 2008, pp. 103–128.

Hite, Katherine, *When the Romance Ended: Leaders of the Chilean Left, 1968–1998*, New York: Columbia University Press, 2000.

Hite, Katherine, "El monumento a Allende y la política chilena," in Elizabeth Jelin and Victoria Langland, Eds., *Monumentos, memoriales y marcas territoriales* Volume 5, Mexico, DF: Siglo XXI, 2003, pp. 19–55.

Hite, Katherine, "Chile's *MarchaRearme* and the Politics of Counter-Commemoration," *Emisférica* 7.2, *Detrás/Después de la Verdad*, Hemispheric Institute, New York University, February 2011.

Hite, Katherine and Cath Collins, "Memorial Fragments, Monumental Silences and Awakenings in the Contemporary Chilean Political Imagination," *Millennium Journal of International Relations*, 38 (2), 2009, pp. 379–400.

Hoffman, Eva, *After Such Knowledge: Memory, History, and the Legacy of the Holocaust*, New York: Public Affairs, 2004.

Huyssen, Andreas, "El arte mnemónico de Marcelo Brodksy/The Mnemonic Art of Marcelo Brodsky," in Marcelo Brodsky, *Nexo: un ensayo fotográfico/A photographic essay*, Buenos Aires: Centro Cultural Recoleta, 2001, pp. 7–11.

Huyssen, Andreas, "Memory Sites in an Expanded Field: The Memory Park in Buenos Aires," in his *Present Pasts: Urban Palimpsests and the Politics of Memory*, Stanford: Stanford University Press, 2003, pp. 94–109.

Jelin, Elizabeth and Victoria Langland, "Introducción. Las marcas territoriales como nexo entre pasado presente," in Jelin and Langland, Eds., *Monumentos, memoriales y marcas territoriales*, Buenos Aires and Madrid: Siglo XXI, 2003, pp. 1–18.

Jelin, Elizabeth, *State Repression and the Labors of Memory*, Minneapolis, MN: University of Minnesota Press, 2003.

Jelin, Elizabeth, *Los trabajos de la memoria*, Buenos Aires, Argentina: Siglo XXI, 2002.

Joignant, Alfredo, *Un día distinto: Memorias festivas y batallas conmemorativas en torno al 11 de septiembre en Chile 1974–2006*, Santiago: Editorial Universitaria 2007.

Kahane, Claire, "Dark Mirrors: A Feminist Reflection on Holocaust Narrative and the Maternal Metaphor," in Elisabeth Bronfen and Misha Kavka, Eds., *Feminist Consequences: Gender and Culture*, New York: Columbia University Press, 2000, pp. 161–188.

Kaiser, Susana, *Postmemories of Terror: A New Generation Copes with the Legacy of the "Dirty War,"* New York: Palgrave Macmillan, 2005.

Kent, Peter C., "The Vatican and the Spanish Civil War," *European History Quarterly*, 16 (4), October 1986, pp. 441–464.

Kornbluh, Peter, *Pinochet File: A Declassified Dossier on Atrocity and Accountability*, New York: The New Press, 2004.

Krog, Antjie, *Country of My Skull: Guilt, Sorrow, and the Limits of Forgiveness in the New South Africa*, New York: Three Rivers Press, 2000.

Lanusse, Lucas. *Montoneros: El mito de sus 12 fundadores*. Buenos Aires, Argentina: Vergara, 2006.

Laub, Dori, "Truth and Testimony: The Process and the Struggle," in Cathy Caruth, Ed., *Trauma: Explorations in Memory*. Baltimore, MD, 1995, pp. 61–75.

Lazarra, Michael, *Chile in Transition: The Poetics and Politics of Memory*, Gainesville, FL: University Press of Florida, 2006.

Lewis, C.S., *A Grief Observed*, San Francisco: Harper Collins, 1961.

Longoni, Ana, "Traiciones. La figura del traidor (y la traidora) en los relatos acerca de los sobreviventes de la repression," in Elizabeth Jelin and Ana Longoni, Eds., *Escrituras, imágenes y escenarios ante la repression*, Buenos Aires: Siglo XXI, 2005, pp. 203–240.

Loveman, Brian, *Chile: The Legacy of Hispanic Capitalism*, New York: Oxford University Press, 1979.

Mannheim, Karl, "The Problem of Generations," in Paul Kecskemeti, Ed., *Essays on the Sociology of Knowledge*, New York: Oxford University Press, 1928, pp. 286–322.

Mason, Carol, *Killing for Life: The Apocalyptic Narrative of Pro-Life Politics*, Ithaca, NY: Cornell University Press, 2002.

Maureira, Juan René, "Enfrentar con la vida la muerte: Historia y memorias de la violencia y el Terrorismo de Estado en Paine (1960–2008)," www.cybertesis.cl/tesis/uchile/2009/maureira_j/html/index-frames.html (accessed July 24, 2011).

Mignolo, Walter D., *Local Histories/Global Designs: Coloniality, Subaltern Knowledges, and Border Thinking*, Princeton, NJ: Princeton University Press, 2000.

Milton, Cynthia, "Defacing Memory: (Un)tying Peru's Memory Knots," *Memory Studies*, forthcoming.

Mosse, George L., *Fallen Soldiers: Reshaping the Memory of the World Wars*, New York: Oxford University Press, 1990.

Nino, Carlos, *Radical Evil on Trial*, New Haven, CT: Yale University Press, 1996.

Nora, Pierre, "Between Memory and History: Les Lieux de Mémoire," *Representations*, 26, Spring 1989, pp. 7–25.

Núñez Díaz-Balart, Mirta, *Los años del terror: La estrategia de dominio y represión del general Franco*, Madrid: La esfera de los Libros, S.L., 2004.

Oberti, Alejandra, "La flexion del sí mismo en las interpretaciones de la violencia política," Segundo Congreso Internacional Comunicación y Política, Universidad Metropolitana Xochimilco, México, November 2005, www.elortiba.org/oberti.html (accessed September 27, 2010).

Ocaranza, Nicolás, "Rangue: Del latifundio al Chile posdictatorial," in Andrés Baeza, Andrés Estefane, Juan Luis Ossa, Joaquín Fernández, Cristóbal García-Huidobro, Nicolás Ocaranza, and Pablo Moscoso, *XX: Historias del siglo veinte*, Santiago: Grupo Zeta, 2008, pp. 303–399.

Olick, Jeffrey K. and Joyce Robins, "Social Memory Studies: From 'Collective Memory' to the Historical Sociology of Mnemonic Practices," *Annual Review of Sociology*, 24, 1998, pp. 105–140.

Olin, Margaret, "The Winter Garden and Virtual Heaven," in Robert S. Nelson and Margaret Olin, *Monuments and Memory, Made and Unmade*, Chicago: University of Chicago Press, 2003, pp. 133–155.

Olmeda, Fernando, *El Valle de los Caídos: Una memoria de España*, Madrid: Ediciones Peninsula, 2009.

Oyarzún, Pablo, Richard, Nelly, and Zaldivar, Claudia, *Arte y política*, Santiago, Chile: Universidad Arcis, 2005.

Payne, Stanley, *The Franco Regime: 1936–1975*, Madison, WI: University of Wisconsin, 1987.

Pérez de Urbel, Don Justo, *El monumento de Santa Cruz del Valle de los Caídos*, Madrid: Instituto de Estudios Madrileños, 1959.

Piper, Isabel, "Obstinaciones de la memoria: la dictadura military chilena en las tramas del recuerdo," Doctoral Thesis in Social Psychology, Autonomous University of Barcelona, Spain, 2005.

Portelli, Alessandro, *The Death of Luigi Trastulli and Other Stories: Form and Meaning in Oral History*, Albany, NY: SUNY Press, 1991.

Report of the Chilean National Commission on Truth and Reconciliation, trans. by Phillip E. Berryman, Volume 1, South Bend, IN: University of Notre Dame Press.

Rothberg, Michael, *Multidirectional Memory: Remembering the Holocaust in the Age of Decolonization*, Stanford, CA: Stanford University Press, 2009.

Sánchez-Albornoz, Nicolás, "Cuelgamuros: presos políticos para un mausoleo," Mexico, D.F., Mexico: CEMOS 2003.

Sancho, José Luis, *Guide to the Santa Cruz del Valle de los Caídos*, Madrid: Patrimonio Nacional, 2003.

Savage, Kirk, "The Politics of Memory: Black Emancipation and the Civil War Monument," in John R. Gillis, Ed., *Commemorations: The Politics of National Identity*, Princeton, NJ: Princeton University Press, 1994, pp. 127–149.

Scarry, Elaine, *The Body in Pain: The Making and Unmaking of the World*, New York: Oxford University Press, 1985.

Senior, Jennifer, "The Prozac, Paxil, Zoloft, Wellbutrin, Celexa, Effexor, Valium, Klonopin, Ativan, Restoril, Xanax, Adderall, Ritalin, Haldol, Risperdal, Seroquel, Ambien, Lunesta, Elavil, Trazodone War," *New York*, February 14, 2011.

Sherman, Daniel J., "Bodies and Names: The Emergence of Commemoration in Interwar France," *American Historical Review*, April 1998, 103, pp. 443–466.

Silva, Emilio and Santiago Macías, *Las fosas de Franco: Los republicanos que el dictador dejó en las cunetas*, Madrid: Editorial Temas de Hoy, 2003.

Silva, Emilio, Asunción Esteban, Javier Castán, and Pancho Salvador, *La memoria de los olvidados: Un debate sobre el silencio de la represión franquista*, Madrid: Ambito Ediciones, 2004.

Santiago Sondereguer, María, "El debate sobre el pasado reciente en Argentina," *Punto de Vista* XXIX (87), December 2000.

Sontag, Susan, *Regarding the Pain of Others*, New York: Picador, 2003.

Sturken, Marita and James E. Young, "Monuments," *Encyclopedia of Aesthetics*, Volume 3, Oxford: Oxford University Press, 1998.

Sturken, Marita, "The Remembering of Forgetting: Recovered Memory and the Question of Experience," *Social Text*, 57 (Winter), 1998, pp. 103–125.

Sturken, Marita, "The Wall, the Screen, and the Image: The Vietnam Veterans Memorial," *Representations*, 35, 1991, pp. 118–142.

Sturken, Marita, *Tangled Memories: The Vietnam War, the AIDS Epidemic, and the Politics of Remembering*, Berkeley, CA: University of California Press, 1997.

Sturken, Marita, *Tourists of History: Memory, Kitsch, and Consumerism from Oklahoma City to Ground Zero*, Durham, NC: Duke University Press, 2007.

Sueiro, Daniel, *La verdadera historia del Valle de los Caídos*, Madrid: SEDMAY Ediciones, 1977.

Sulca, Aroni and Salvador, Renzo, "'Aprendimos a convivir con los senderistas y militares': violencia política y respuesta campesina en Huamanquiquia, 1980–1993," *Investigaciones Sociales* X (17), 2006, pp. 261–284.

Surtz, Ronald, Jaime Ferrán, and Daniel Testa, Eds., *Américo Castro: The Impact of His Thought: Essays to Mark the Centenary of His Birth*, Madison, WI: University of Wisconsin Press, 1988.

Taylor, Diana, *Disappearing Acts: Spectacles of Gender and Nationalism in Argentina's "Dirty War,"* Durham, NC: Duke University Press, 1997.

Taylor, Diana, *The Archive and the Repertoire: Performing Cultural Memory in the Americas*, Durham, NC: Duke University Press, 2003.

Theidon, Kimberly, *Entre prójmos: el conflicto armado interno y la política de la reconciliación en el Perú*, Lima: IEP, 2004.

Theidon, Kimberly, "Justice in Transition: The Micropolitics of Reconciliation in Postwar Peru," *Journal of Conflict Resolution*, 50 (3), 2006, pp. 433–457.

Todorov, Tzvetan, *Les abus de la mémoire*, París: Arléa, 1998.

Valdez, Patricia, "El Parque de la Memoria en Buenos Aires," in Elizabeth Jelin and Victoria Langland, Eds., *Monumentos, memoriales y marcas territoriales*, Buenos Aires and Madrid: Siglo XXI, 2003, pp. 97–111.

Valenzuela, Arturo, *The Breakdown of Democratic Regimes: Chile*, Baltimore, MD: Johns Hopkins University Press, 1979.

Verdugo, Patricia, *Tiempo de días claros: los desaparecidos*, Santiago, Chile: CESOC, 1990.

Weitzel, Ruby, *El callejón de las viudas*, Santiago: Editorial Planeta, 2001.

Young, James E., *The Texture of Memory: Holocaust Memorials and Meaning*, New Haven, CT: Yale University Press, 1993.

Young, James, "The Counter-Monument: Memory Against Itself in Germany Today," *Critical Inquiry*, Winter 1992, 18 (2), pp. 267–296.

Young, James, "Memory Against Itself in Germany Today: Jochen Gerz's Counter-monuments," in James Young, Ed., *At Memory's Edge: After-Images of the Holocaust in Contemporary Art and Architecture*, New Haven, CT: Yale University Press, 2000, pp. 120–151.

Youngers, Coletta, *Violencia política y sociedad civil en el Perú: Historia de la Coordinadora Nacional de Derechos Humanos*, Lima: Instituto de Estudios Peruanos, 2003.

Youngers, Coletta, "La promoción de los derechos humanos: las ongs y el estado en el Perú," in John Crabtree, Ed., *Construir instituciones: democracia, desarrollo, y desigualdad en el Perú desde 1980*, Lima: Fondo Editorial de la Pontificia Universidad Católica del Perú, Universidad del Pacífico, y el Instituto de Estudios Peruanos, 2006, pp. 163–188.

Cited interviews

Marcelo Brodsky
Doris Caqui
Rubén Chababo
Juan Leonardo Maureira
Juan René Maureira
Lika Mutal
Rosario Narváez
Javier Roca Obregón
Gabriela Ortíz
Fernando Traverso

Index